★ INSIDE THE ★
WHITE
HOUSE

★ INSIDE THE ★
WHITE HOUSE

AMERICA'S MOST FAMOUS HOME
THE FIRST 200 YEARS

★ BETTY BOYD CAROLI ★

CANOPY BOOKS

a division of Abbeville Press

NEW YORK

Book design, jacket, endsheets, and binding:
Richard Kopyscianski, Creative Director
Art Direction by Diana Klemin

Front endsheet:
Eubie Blake playing ragtime on the South Lawn.
Back endsheet:
Olympics winners at the White House.
Frontispiece:
North front of the White House.

Front jacket photographs: President Kennedy with son John Jr.; courtesy of John F. Kennedy Library. Eleanor Roosevelt with Queen Elizabeth, 1939; courtesy of Franklin D. Roosevelt Library. President Bush with granddaughters; courtesy of Susan Biddle, The White House. President Truman; courtesy of AP/Wide World Photos. President Ford with Queen Elizabeth II; courtesy of Gerald R. Ford Library. President Lyndon Johnson with Courtney Valenti; courtesy of Lyndon B. Johnson Library. Nancy Reagan; courtesy of White House Historical Association/National Geographic. Back jacket: South view of White House; courtesy of White House Historical Association.

Second Canopy Books edition

Published by The Reader's Digest Association, Inc., 1994, by permission of Doubleday Book & Music Clubs, Inc.

Library of Congress Cataloging-in-Publication Data
Caroli, Betty Boyd.
   Inside the White House; America's most famous home, the first 200 years/Betty Boyd Caroli.
   p. cm.
   Includes bibliographical references and index.
   ISBN 1-55859-818-9
   1. White House (Washington, D.C.)   2. Presidents—United States—History.   3. Washington (D.C.)—Buildings, structures, etc.
I. Title.
F204.W5C27   1992
975.3—dc20   92-14399
                                                             CIP

For my mother, Edna Henry Boyd
and the memory of my father, Clyde Ford Boyd

CONTENTS

FOREWORD

Telling the White House story is not easy, nor can one book do it all. Dozens of volumes have already been written on topics as diverse as White House food and pets, architecture and music, gardens and furniture, glassware and automobiles. The occupants themselves and the building's staff have published countless memoirs about the time they spent in the White House, and historians and journalists have provided their own accounts (sometimes exposés) of what happened there.

Rather than duplicate any of these previous efforts, this book focuses on what the White House has come to mean at the time of its two hundredth birthday—the roles it plays and the uses it serves. Eleanor Roosevelt once titled an article "The White House Speaks" —she seemed to understand that the building took its own measure, confident of its own significance and permanence. More than simply surviving shifts in political thinking, the White House grows in prominence regardless of the criticism leveled at its occupants.

Organized thematically in four sections, the pages that follow go inside the White House in something other than a physical sense. Photographs, chosen from among countless available, have been selected to illustrate the four themes and show alterations over time. Readers will get a good idea of what the mansion looks like for its bicentennial celebration, but they will also understand the route it followed to achieve that look.

Readers who want more extensive coverage of any one topic will need to consult the list of additional readings on page 217. The volumes by William Seale, Elise Kirk, Jane Shadel Spillman, and Margaret Klapthor, as well as the White House guidebooks published and richly illustrated by the White House Historical Association, will be particularly useful. They prepared me for examining

In the era of bustles and parasols, before security considerations caused it to be closed off, the South Lawn provided a good vantage point for viewing White House residents who appeared on the South Portico.

documents at the White House, the Library of Congress, and the Houghton Library of Harvard University.

I have had generous assistance from many people. At the White House, Associate Curator Betty Monkman brought out files for me to look at and made other arrangements that facilitated the research. She and others in the White House Curator's Office, especially Assistant Curator William Allman and Angela Horton, answered countless questions and commented on portions of the manuscript. Staffs at the presidential libraries, Library of Congress, White House Historical Association, and White House Photo Offices cheerfully cooperated with me to find pictures. At Doubleday Book Clubs, an enthusiastic team, including Richard Kopyscianski, Diana Klemin, Barbara Greenman, Al Stiene, Joanne Willig, and Eleanor Tilvikas made my work a pleasure. Mary Sherwin Jatlow, Senior Editor, merits special thanks—for realizing that the White House bicentennial deserved a book and for her patience and good humor in seeing the project through.

INTRODUCTION
The White House: Two Hundred Years

After months of talk, the time had come to act, and the group that had gathered outside the Georgetown, Maryland tavern began walking southeast. In the lead were members of the local Masonic Lodge, whose fellow Mason, General George Washington, could not join them that Saturday—duties as President of the new United States of America detained him in Philadelphia. But Washington's wishes were very much on the men's minds—he had personally selected the spot where they were heading. There on a pleasant wooded knoll overlooking the Potomac River a home would be built for future Presidents of the nation: these men were going to lay the cornerstone for the White House.

It is doubtful that any of the Masons, stonecutters, or others who came together that October day in 1792 could have imagined the interest their actions would arouse two hundred years later. Only one newspaper account—from South Carolina—survives, and it does not record exactly where the cornerstone was placed. Most informed guesses put it somewhere on the southwest corner.

A drawing of the President's House after its burning in August 1814.

This photograph of the White House is one of the earliest known.

Ebullient over their accomplishment, the men returned to the Georgetown tavern and drank a toast to the future, but never in their wildest dreams could they have foreseen what the President's House would become. They could not have conceived that it would eventually add a bomb shelter to its basement and computer screens to every office; that one million visitors would walk through its rooms every year; and that live broadcasts would electronically transmit its picture around the world.

Had they been able to see into the future, the builders of the White House might have opted for a larger structure. George Washington would not have objected—he approved of the idea that Presidents should reside in style, and the city planner he selected in 1791, Frenchman Pierre L'Enfant, envisioned an American capital with majestic stone buildings and wide boulevards lined with fountains and monuments. The President's House in L'Enfant's plan would be enormous, about five times the size of the one eventually built.

Washington's approval, although very important, did not suffice to permit L'Enfant to proceed against the opposition of other Americans who wanted something more modest. Thomas Jefferson, who as Secretary of State had an important role in building the new Federal City, envisioned a setting that emphasized natural elements —rolling hills and small streams—like his beloved Monticello in Charlottesville. The three Commissioners selected to oversee the building project agreed with Jefferson—they had doubts about how Americans would react to a palace. Congress failed to appropriate any funds for L'Enfant, and then Jefferson fired him.

Now it was February 1792, and quick action was required. Thomas Jefferson suggested holding a contest to collect ideas for the President's House, and within months, nine entries came in. This was hardly an outpouring of enthusiasm in a nation numbering nearly four million people. Architects in Philadelphia and New York ignored the contest as though they considered it beneath their consideration, and Boston's renowned Charles Bulfinch declined to enter "on the grounds of modesty." But from among the nine proposals, one stood out and was quickly accepted by the Commissioners, perhaps because it had fewer of the features associated

Elaborate conservatories built in the 1850s provided presidential families with fresh flowers and a place to walk after dinner.

with a palace. The other entries, including some with large central courts and one with space for a draped throne, lost out to that of James Hoban who had been building homes for wealthy planters in South Carolina.

Historians would later agree that James Hoban's entry was not original, but then originality was not one of the requirements. He borrowed heavily from examples in his native Dublin: Leinster House (later House of Parliament) and the Lying-In Hospital both had Palladian façades and windows hooded in triangular shapes like those that would grace some of the windows in the President's House. When John Kennedy visited Ireland in 1963, he joked about how much the White House resembled "Dublin style" and concluded that James Hoban had wanted to make American Presidents of Irish descent feel at home. "It was a long wait," quipped Kennedy, "but I appreciate his efforts." Then the American President speculated on the rumor that Hoban had not been "fully paid."

Original or not, Hoban's design meshed nicely with the new nation's ideas about itself—simple in line yet big enough to qualify as the largest home in the nation. After George Washington prevailed on Hoban to add some stone embellishments to the exterior, take away the third floor, and increase the dimensions by one-fifth, building could begin. This would enable the cornerstone to be laid on October 13, 1792, just a bit behind schedule.

L'Enfant's plan for a stone structure survived, and Hoban took charge of construction. The surrounding area could not supply the workmen needed, and a call went out to other states (and even Europe) for help. Before it was finished many nationalities would help in the construction of the President's House, and although a complete roster of them does not exist, historians estimate that about one-half of those employed were foreign-born. The Irishman Hoban took up where the Frenchman L'Enfant left off, working alongside the Scottish stonemason Collen Williamson and other Scotsmen and many African-Americans hired by the day.

Eight years after the cornerstone was laid, John and Abigail Adams moved in. It should be noted that the exterior of the White House at that time had not yet achieved the look that we know today. Thomas Jefferson oversaw the addition of low wings to the east and west; James Monroe presided over the building of the rounded portico on the south; Andrew Jackson added a rectangular portico on the north. But over the years the four exterior walls—measuring 165 feet from east to west and 85 feet from north to

An office building—the West Wing of the White House —replaced the conservatories in 1902.

Over the years intricate stonework was covered up by dozens of layers of white paint so that in the 1980s a thorough cleaning was required to reveal its detail.

south—have retained their original dimensions and placement against every intrusion and change in occupants.

By the 1940s, the White House exterior had taken on icon status, as President Harry Truman learned when he suggested adding a second floor to the South Portico. Defending the change on both aesthetic and historic grounds, he insisted the porch offered an improvement over the current arrangement in which awnings, used to shut out the sun, became soiled and torn. Many Americans objected loudly to tampering with the White House façade but in the end, Truman got his way. Several of his successors, including Richard Nixon, spoke out in defense of the "Truman porch," but it caused some difficulty at the United States Mint: the engraving of the White House on twenty-dollar bills had to be redone.

The interior of the White House proved less impervious to alteration, and the basic structure incurred considerable weakening as one modern convenience after another was imposed on it: walls were cut up to accommodate gas pipes and electric wires; bathrooms and elevators took their toll.

In 1949, President Truman received warnings about the building's structural weaknesses that were even more alarming than those that had prompted a general renovation in 1902. Margaret Truman's piano had started to go through the floor, breaking the ceiling on a state room below, and the Commissioner of Public Buildings, W. E. Reynolds, was quoted as saying that the second floor "was staying up there purely from habit."

Thus began an enormous project taking more than three years in which the White House structure would be reinforced and its space expanded, while the basic four walls would not be budged even one inch. This remarkable feat was accomplished by gutting the interior and then installing a new steel frame inside. A renovation in 1927 had already added a third floor, recessed and concealed from public view by a balustrade. The 1949 modernization went in another direction to accomplish further expansion without visibly altering the exterior: excavating under the old basement. By 1952, when the Truman project was completed, the official total of rooms was set at 132, of which thirty-five are considered "principal."

The same stubbornness that protected the four walls from dem-

In 1927 extensive work on the White House provided more living space on the third floor that had previously been used for service and storage areas.

In 1949–52, the interior of the White House was completely gutted, and a steel frame was assembled inside the original stone walls.

olition and relocation also affected the naming of the building. Although it was originally known as the President's House (and that is how its flatware and linens were marked), references to the "white house" cropped up almost as soon as the gray sandstone was covered with its first coat of whitewash in 1798. After being rebuilt, following the burning by the British troops in the War of 1812, it was gradually renamed "Executive Mansion" (the word "mansion" commonly used in the nineteenth century to describe homes of wealthy citizens). But Americans persisted in calling it the "White House," and finally, in 1902, Theodore Roosevelt made that name the official one. He explained that every state had an Executive Mansion and the President of the United States deserved a residence of unique title.

Much about the White House went beyond an ordinary executive's home. Even before its site was selected, George Washington had decided that he would live and work at the same address. His successors followed his lead in spite of their own misgivings and

17

the loud objections of their families. First Lady Edith Roosevelt likened the arrangement to a storekeeper "living above the store," and President Chester Arthur insisted no businessman would tolerate it: "You have no idea," he once told a reporter, "how depressing and fatiguing it is to live in the same house where you work."

As though the dual burden of serving as both home and office were not enough for one building, the White House gradually took on a third role—national museum. Special importance attached itself to the contents of the President's House: its glassware, china, and furniture attained exceptional value and aroused great interest. Americans who wanted the best examples of their nation's workmanship to grace the President's House donated prized furniture and art to it, and visitors lined up to see the exhibits. In 1988 the American Association of Museums accredited the White House as a museum.

The fourth role of the Executive Mansion, as the People's House, has been obvious and frequently acknowledged. From the beginning, Americans deemed it their property: they paid the bills and they meant to call the tune. Public tours throughout the year, enormous receptions for thousands of invited guests, concerts, and Christmas parties brought many people inside; crowds gathered on their own outside the gates to shout in victory when wars ended and protest in anger against policies they did not like.

What began as a relatively modest estate on the Potomac—a home for the President—has evolved in two hundred years into a national symbol of the first order. Unlike other important monuments such as the Statue of Liberty that speak to one part of the nation's past, the White House speaks to many. As home-office-museum-gathering place, it plays four roles in the nation's history, four parts on the world's stage. Any one of them would suffice to make the White House special; together they assure its unique importance and guarantee that millions of people will want to go inside.

In April 1989 George and Barbara Bush greeted visitors on the North Portico (with parts of the still unpainted north façade behind them).

HOME TO A FAMILY

★ Behind the pomp of diplomatic visits and state dinners, amidst the planning for public tours and cabinet meetings, the White House serves as home to the President and his family. Protocol and international crises are interwoven into the fabric of family life—marriages and anniversaries, births and deaths, illnesses and convalescences. Every President's family, except George Washington's, has lived at 1600 Pennsylvania Avenue (ranging from William Henry Harrison for only one month to Franklin Roosevelt for twelve years), and every occupant, no matter how short his residence there, has had to adjust to a multi-purpose White House.

To the uninitiated observer, a mansion of this size might seem to be able to accommodate easily the dual roles of home and

President Kennedy walks with his young son, John, Jr., outside the Oval Office.

office—in fact, its management resembles that of a small hotel more than a private residence. By 1991 the White House boasted a budget of about seven million dollars and a staff of one hundred and three, including sixteen maids and housemen, seven butlers, nine cooks, and five ushers. To keep the building in tiptop shape, the mansion relies on ten engineers, four carpenters, six electricians, two plumbers, two storekeepers, two painters, and five florists. Additional employees come in on a part-time basis, and the National Park Service takes full responsibility for care of the grounds.

No wonder each incoming First Lady takes a tour of the premises before moving in. Traditionally, since 1909, the outgoing First Lady has introduced her successor to the mansion, and only rarely has she delegated the task to an assistant. Even personal inconvenience need not delay this visit. Just days after she had delivered a son by Caesarean section, Jacqueline Kennedy accompanied Mamie Eisenhower through dozens of White House rooms in order to make plans for moving in. Three years later Mrs. Kennedy went over housekeeping details with Lady Bird Johnson—one day after John Kennedy's funeral.

Even when the President and his family have campaigned in a bitterly contested election and lost, the tour takes place. Such events can be bittersweet, as when Lou Hoover, deeply disappointed that voters had rejected her husband's bid for reelection in 1932, walked with Eleanor Roosevelt through the family quarters on the second floor, or as when Rosalynn Carter, despondent after her husband's 1980 presidential defeat, escorted Nancy Reagan through the family section.

As each new President and his family move in, arrangements are made for the living quarters to suit their comfort. Betty Ford planned so that she and her husband had one room they could "crawl into and shut the door." She wanted their own favorite things there—the President's old blue leather chair, exercise bike, pipes and pipe rack. The valuable antiques in the White House collection were lovely but, like a lodger in the most finely appointed hotel, she insisted on a private space that she and her husband could call their own.

Most transitions from one administration to the next are sharp and precise. Clothing, personal furnishings, even pampered pets

In August 1974, before they moved in, Betty Ford joined her daughter Susan in a tour of the family quarters of the White House.

are all moved out, their substitutions in place in a matter of hours. All this is accomplished with very little fanfare. Back in 1909, Helen Taft noted that there is "never any ceremony about moving into the White House. You just drive up and walk in."

Within weeks of the change in administration, the domestic staff can feel an altered atmosphere—casual and friendly, or restrained and more formal—as bedrooms and sitting rooms on the second floor are rearranged to reflect their new occupants. Some families make few changes, bringing in only their most essential personal possessions—a favorite bed or special photographs— while other presidential families transform the upstairs quarters, installing new wallpaper and rugs. Color preferences are obvious: Mamie Eisenhower liked lots of pink, and Nancy Reagan's personal favorite was red.

What one family considers essential, the next one may discard. Lyndon Johnson insisted on shower heads that delivered a forceful spray but his successor, Richard Nixon, had them removed. The Hoovers added thirteen radios, many telephones, and matched furniture, while the Roosevelts just wanted "something comfortable."

Sometimes, having lived abroad or traveled extensively, the President and First Lady show their preference for a "foreign" flavor in furnishings. In 1911 *Good Housekeeping* described the Taft White House as "Oriental," with "cunningly carved teakwood chairs, tables, cabinets, and wonderful Eastern fabrics," all evidence of the Tafts' years in the Philippines. The Hoovers arrived with a sizable collection of Chinese vases, and Ellen Wilson, although she had never lived in Asia, redecorated the dark central hall in straw-colored Japanese paper. Nearly seventy years later Nancy Reagan brought her own special collection of tiny Chinese porcelain vases for display in the West Sitting Hall.

Besides an experienced staff to oversee the moving-in of the President and his family and the redecoration of the second-floor quarters, there are other enormous perquisites of White House living. After two years as First Lady, Barbara Bush told a reporter: "You'd have to be a little crazy not to like this." Former residents have recalled the thrill of traveling in limousines and private planes, arriving by helicopter on the South Lawn. The Fords' daughter Susan compared the whole experience to living "a fairy

Lyndon Johnson, who reportedly spent many hours on the telephone every day, speaks here from the West Sitting Hall on the second floor while daughter Lynda and grandson Patrick Lyndon Nugent look on.

The East Sitting Hall also serves as a place to entertain personal guests.

Lady Bird Johnson wheels her grandson on the South Lawn, August 1967.

tale," and Lyndon Johnson's daughters talked of the excitement of meeting movie stars and world leaders every week. On one occasion in 1964 Lynda Bird, still a college student, helped host a lawn party where guests included Leonard Bernstein, Helen Hayes, George Balanchine, Willem de Kooning, Harper Lee, Walter Lippmann, Marya Mannes, Dr. J. Robert Oppenheimer, Ben Shahn, and many others equally famous. Luci Johnson, Lynda's younger sister, called White House living "a unique opportunity," one that anybody who had the chance should "savor" because "nothing like that will ever pass your way again."

Many White House families, however, feel overwhelmed by all the attention focused on them, and they complain about the lack of privacy. "Normal" routines now fall under the control of teams of staff members who schedule the family's mornings, afternoons, and evenings.

Most Presidents' families have never before lived in such a large residence and they must make their own rules about how to act around the domestic staff. The Nixons instructed employees to be as invisible and silent as possible, while Betty Ford wanted to be answered when she said "Good morning," and at "strictly family meals" President Ford liked to compare golf scores with the butler. The Hoovers, who were accustomed to having many servants in their homes in China and London, were often deemed cool and detached by White House staff members, while the Coolidges, who had always lived in modest rented quarters, treated the domestic staff almost as family.

Lack of privacy is perhaps the biggest complaint of Presidents' families. Sometimes the White House seems to have no walls, and as the ultimate "glass house," its every inch is considered open for viewing. In the early 1900s Edith Roosevelt noted that security agents watched her closely, even when she sat out on the porch. They must have thought, she observed wryly, that "I was about to hatch anarchists." Almost sixty years later Jacqueline Kennedy objected to losing her anonymity at the age of thirty-one when she became First Lady, and she tried hard to protect her two young children from reporters. Caroline, at age five, learned to hold up a warning hand and say, "No photographs." Lady Bird Johnson retreated to a small sitting room that had the virtue of "only one door," and she kept a little cushion to hang on the doorknob—tellingly imprinted, "I want to be alone."

This complaint about inadequate privacy was no twentieth-century development. In the 1840s the Polks, who had no children of their own, invited a niece, Joanna Rucker, for lengthy visits to the White House, and she wrote to a cousin in Tennessee that she was always being interrupted by some straggler who would pretend to lose his way to the President's office and stumble into the private family quarters. She laid the blame on the fact that the house belonged "to the Government and everyone feels at home."

Past residents of the Executive Mansion have also acknowledged the cost of putting one's life on hold as educations are shelved, friends distanced, hobbies and personal travel curtailed under the pressures of White House life. In 1964 Luci Johnson was only seventeen but she gave up her own social life to campaign for her father's reelection. Every weekend (except one) for about six months, she left the White House to go out and speak in his behalf. "From Friday noon until Sunday evening," there were, she recalled, "no dates and no parties." Once she escaped into a White House closet after hearing her mother and a presidential aide discuss sending her out to campaign on a weekend when she had already scheduled two dates.

Rosalynn Carter remembered that living in the White House changed the way people treated her. "Even my best friends looked at me differently," she admitted, and those who came to visit her in the White House were so in awe of the building that she found herself struggling to put them at ease. Susan Ford put it differently: the White House brings you "new friends," she said, and you have to be "cautious."

★★★

In that large house at 1600 Pennsylvania Avenue even the definition of the word "family" sometimes changes. The multiple facets of the President's job—social, political, executive—have encouraged the practice of inviting individuals outside the immediate family circle to serve in a supportive role. Widower Thomas Jefferson initiated the practice when he invited his married daughter, Martha Jefferson Randolph, to bring her family to stay in the Executive Mansion while her husband served in the U.S. Senate. The Presi-

Kennedy children, Caroline and John, Jr., join their father in the colonnade connecting the residence to the West Wing.

President Bush pauses to pose with granddaughters on his way to the West Wing.

dent also employed as secretaries two young men, Meriwether Lewis and William Clark, who worked and slept in a section of the East Room while Jefferson tutored them for their western expedition.

Martin Van Buren, whose wife had died nearly two decades before he assumed the presidency in 1837, took along his four sons when he moved into the Executive Mansion. Ranging from twenty to thirty years of age, they assisted their father in various ways, and the eldest, Abraham, served as his father's private secretary. In 1838 Abraham married Angelica Singleton, a relative of Dolley Madison, and he brought his bride to live at the White House where she presided as surrogate First Lady for the rest of President Van Buren's term.

Extended families residing in the White House—married sons and daughters, grandchildren and in-laws—came to be frowned on in the late twentieth century, as though voters objected to the cost or the privilege. Exceptions occurred, of course—Bess Truman's mother made lengthy visits to the White House and died there in 1952—but most presidential households in the twentieth century did not include the many relatives that were common earlier when voters approved, even applauded, this evidence that their leader was a solid family man. The only bachelor President, James Buchanan, was frequently written off as unfit for the job.

John Tyler eventually fathered fifteen children by two wives, more than any other President, and eight of them were born before he was called upon to lead the nation in 1841. The youngest son, then eleven years old, and three teen-aged daughters might have been expected to live with their parents, but President Tyler also arranged for his adult children and their spouses to live in the White House. The wife of Tyler's oldest son, Robert—an actress who appeared on the stage as Priscilla Cooper—often filled in as White House hostess.

Some Americans complained that Abraham Lincoln stretched the White House welcome mat a little too far. While Union forces were fighting a bloody war to put down the rebellion of Confederate states, Lincoln faced a delicate family situation. His wife's relatives were divided, and some of them, including her brothers, supported the South. When the husband of Mary Lincoln's youngest sister was killed in action, his widow, Emilie Helm, needed a place to stay and the President said, "Send her to me." Thus it happened that a Confederate widow slept in the White House while the Civil War continued, and rumors grew about traitors in high places.

Ulysses and Julia Dent Grant both had their fathers stay with them in the White House, and the elder Mr. Grant became famous for quarreling with the aged Mr. Dent. Their verbal assaults on each other, as reported with some glee in the national press, titillated the nation. One would accuse the other of being too deaf to hear anything, and the other would respond with coarser insults.

Sometimes the President's household reached outside the extended family to include employees or close friends in an attempt to make the pressured job of President a little less so. In December 1850, President Fillmore invited his law partner from Buffalo to come stay at the White House, explaining as he did so that it was "a temple of inconveniences" but had one room "neatly fitted up for guests." Franklin and Eleanor Roosevelt hosted several close aides and friends for months at a time. Harry Hopkins, a trusted adviser,

President Truman stopped for this photograph on the way to church on May 13, 1945, the day he set aside for prayerful thanksgiving for the end of the war in Europe. He is joined by his wife Bess, their daughter Margaret, Mrs. Truman's brother Fred Wallace, Mrs. Truman's mother, and the President's sister.

lived there with his daughter after his first wife died, and when he married again he stayed on for more than a year. Lorena Hickok, Eleanor's journalist friend, also had her own room at the White House for years.

★★★

All this activity could not have been predicted by architect James Hoban when he submitted the original plans for the President's House in 1792, but he did understand that this would be no ordinary residence. Like a wealthy planter's home, it featured spacious rooms of grand proportions on the first floor where parties and business meetings could accommodate dozens of guests. Above this "public" or "state" floor, the family's rooms were scaled to private uses—sleeping and family conversation.

Much like a latter-day hotel, the White House has always differentiated its three original floors according to function. Service areas—for food preparation, laundry and heating equipment—were relegated to the basement (actually the ground floor if viewed from the south). The first or "public floor" had large rooms with high ceilings and a grand entrance hall to serve for the most festive occasions, and upstairs on the second floor the family had its living quarters. Even that level had a public air about it, its spacious corridor running from east to west, providing parlor space for bedrooms on both sides.

From the beginning, circumstances encouraged considerable overlap between public and private uses of the mansion. Abigail Adams practically reversed Hoban's design—she invited visitors on business upstairs to the family floor because the first floor remained unfurnished and she requisitioned as a backyard the large East Room, which would later become the setting for the grandest White House social events. Her decision to hang laundry in the large "Audience Room" resulted partly from the season (it was December) but also from considerations of propriety (she recognized the indignity of putting out the President's underwear for all the neighbors to see).

The smaller parlors between the East Room and the Dining Room—later known as the Green Room, the Blue Room, and the Red Room, used for elegant public receptions—also were pressed into personal use by Presidents' families. Thomas Jefferson claimed the Green Room as a dining hall; William Howard Taft transformed

Frances Folsom Cleveland, the only White House bride of a President, sits in the West Hall on the second floor, near the Steinway piano that had been a wedding gift from William Steinway.

Esther Cleveland, the only child of a President ever born in the White House, is held by her mother, Frances Cleveland, while her older sister Ruth looks on.

the Blue Room into a music room, complete with Victrola and record collection; and Theodore Roosevelt's children used the Red Room as a play area and walked on stilts there.

Even with rooms serving dual purposes, the Executive Mansion was considered too small within decades of being built, and in 1857 one newspaper predicted that it would soon be used only for business and official entertaining. The Chief Executive could take his family to live in some more "salubrious" part of the capital city where he would not have to be "perplexed and annoyed at all hours by the crowd of licensed beggars and borers."

The First Family's housing problem worsened in the second half of the nineteenth century when the President's office staff took over the eastern end of the second floor. Large families had to subdivide the few rooms allotted to them in order to have a sufficient number of bedrooms. There were many complaints and several Presidents and their wives threatened to live elsewhere. Julia Grant thought she and her husband should keep their house on "I" Street—the President would commute to 1600 Pennsylvania Avenue for work and official entertaining. But the First Lady soon found that she was dealing with an inviolable tradition and the Grants put the "I" Street house up for sale.

Grover Cleveland was more successful than most Presidents in defying the tradition of residing year-round in the White House. Upon moving in he had found the building badly deteriorated, and although the living quarters were fairly well kept, the rest was shabby and dirty. One of his aides reported that the building had cockroaches; the attic contained "a terrible mess of junk"; and the basement was full of "rubble and overturned ash cans." Just before his marriage in 1886, President Cleveland announced that he needed a refuge so he could "go and be away from this cursed grind." He bought a house and thirty acres of land about three miles north of the mansion and lived there with his bride Frances for much of the year. From December to March when the social calendar peaked, the Clevelands slept at 1600 Pennsylvania Avenue, but in April the family's White House furniture was covered with large cloths, called "wraps," and the Clevelands moved out to their private retreat. The only President to serve two nonconsecutive terms (1885–89, 1893–97), Cleveland made a similar living arrangement

This postcard celebrated the fact that Grover Cleveland—reelected in 1892 after being out of the White House for four years—was the only President to serve two nonconsecutive terms.

Edith Kermit Roosevelt, Theodore Roosevelt's wife, assigned rooms on the west end of the second floor to herself and her husband, daughters Alice and Ethel, and sons Kermit, Quentin, and Archie.

Offices   T's private office

KERMIT | HALL | E.K.R. LIBRARY | GARDEN

TWO MAIDS

GUEST | Quentin ARCHIE

B. AND D' ROOM | B ROOM | LIFT

ALICE | E.K.R

276 | STAIRS

ETHEL | BATH | BATH | T. DRESSING ROOM

for his second term in office. By then he had young children and the privacy of his own home seemed even more important.

The White House, with its large staff, did have some advantages that the Clevelands could not ignore, however, and when First Lady Frances Cleveland was ready to give birth in September 1893, she remained there for the delivery. Her decision proved to be historic—the Clevelands' daughter, Esther, was the only President's child to be born in the mansion in two hundred years.

Benjamin and Caroline Harrison, who followed the Clevelands into the White House in 1889, agreed that they needed more room for their extended family. Because there were too few sitting rooms, at times the First Lady was required to invite female guests into her bedroom for conversation. Three possible solutions providing for more space were put forth. One called for building a separate residence for the President on Sixteenth Street and using the White House only for business and entertaining; the second plan outlined minor additions to the existing structure; and the third proposal, favored by the Harrisons, would have transformed the White House into a grandiose horseshoe with enormous conservatories. A fountain planned for the center courtyard would commemorate Christopher Columbus's arrival in America—thus noting the coincidence of the White House cornerstone being laid on October 13, 1792, the three hundredth anniversary of Columbus's first full day in the New World.

If the third proposal had been accepted, the President's House would look more like a palace than the White House we know today. But Congress balked at spending the money, and the Harrisons, like their predecessors, had to make do with minor renovations and a general cleanup.

Throughout the nineteenth century, Americans seemed content that the President and his family lived simply compared to royalty and heads of other nations. In 1884, a visitor to the White House wrote approvingly: "There is no sham or pretense . . . no effort to look like a temple or a cathedral or a castle. It tries to be a spacious and dignified dwelling and nothing more."

But by 1902, crowding at 1600 Pennsylvania Avenue had become serious. The family of Theodore Roosevelt included six children, ranging in age from seventeen-year-old Alice to four-year-old Quentin. Edith Roosevelt had struggled to divide the five bed-rooms among them but even her best efforts resulted in some doubling up. Each of the Roosevelt daughters had her own space, but the two youngest boys shared a room, as did their brother Kermit whenever older brother Ted, Jr., came home from boarding school.

After the White House underwent a general renovation and refurbishing in 1902, the Roosevelts were able to reclaim the entire second floor as living space and guest quarters. The President retained an office in the residence but his staff moved to the separate, newly built West Wing. Business entertaining and official functions would be confined to the first and ground floors. Important guests might be invited to sleep on the second floor, and small confer-

Theodore Roosevelt's two young sons Archie and Quentin line up with White House police.

ences would occur there, but from this point on, the President's family considered "upstairs" to be their territory.

In 1927 renovations on the third floor provided several more rooms for the family and their personal guests. Formerly used only for utility functions, the top floor was recessed to make fourteen sleeping rooms, several bathrooms, and storage space. This upper floor, with its obvious advantage of being more distant from the public areas, became the choice of young residents. When Betty Ford toured the mansion prior to moving in, she suggested that her daughter use a room on the second floor, across from that of the President and First Lady. Susan, however, much preferred the privacy of a suite on the third floor—the same one that had been used by Julie and David Eisenhower during the Nixon years in the White House.

One area of the third floor became particularly popular. The sun porch or "sky parlor" built on the roof of the South Portico gave unobstructed views of many of the capital's monuments. Shielded from curious eyes, the President's family could enjoy a rare treat—privacy and sunshine at the same time. Margaret Truman played table tennis with her mother there and Bess Truman sometimes hit Ping-Pong balls into the skylight. Lyndon and Lady Bird Johnson's daughters, Luci and Lynda, entertained their young friends in that room, and when Luci married, the bridesmaids' party was held there. Eight years later, on the evening before Richard Nixon resigned the presidency, he and the First Lady

On the evening before Richard Nixon announced to the nation his decision to resign the office of President, his family joined him in the Solarium for this photograph.

Rosalynn Carter enjoyed the sunny views from the Solarium on the third floor of the White House.

assembled in the Solarium with their daughters and sons-in-law.

Even before the third floor was added in 1927, Presidents' families found a measure of privacy on the second floor. Several nineteenth century First Ladies spent so much time there that they became virtually invisible and Washingtonians would not have recognized them if they had walked down the street. Margaret Taylor, whose husband Zachary Taylor served little more than a year as President (1849–50), rarely ventured downstairs, and false rumors circulated to the effect that she smoked a pipe. Eliza Johnson, Mary Lincoln's successor as First Lady, saw almost no one outside her own immediate family. Jane Pierce, distraught over the death of her ten-year-old son just weeks before her husband's inauguration in

35

On Sunday evenings the Hayes family gathered in the second-floor Oval Room to sing hymns. *Frank Leslie's Illustrated Newspaper* **pictured them in its April 3, 1880, issue.**

1853, declined to go downstairs to attend public receptions. (Bennie, the last surviving son of the Pierces—two others had died earlier—had suffered mortal injuries in a train accident, from which both his parents emerged unhurt.)

While twentieth century White House residents abandoned attempts to isolate themselves on the second floor, they did persist in using the family rooms according to patterns set by their predecessors. The second-floor Oval Room remained a favorite, its central position and gracious proportions making it the preferred gathering spot for two centuries. Abigail Adams made it a priority to furnish this room, and her successor Dolley Madison settled on a color scheme that later became permanent: she chose yellow damask for the furniture and curtains.

In 1850 Abigail Fillmore put the family library in the upstairs Oval Room, and her daughter moved in a harp for evenings of music. Twenty-five years later the Hayeses sang hymns there; and in the 1930s and 1940s Franklin Roosevelt, whose mobility was limited, used it as a kind of salon, mixing business and social visits. In the same room, the Lyndon Johnsons celebrated their grandson Lyn's birthday and put up the family Christmas tree.

Most Presidents have chosen to sleep in the suite of rooms on the southwest corner of the second floor. From there they have a long, expansive view out over the South Lawn. The morning sun cannot reach them at dawn, and they are protected a bit from the street noise of Pennsylvania Avenue on the north. During the 1991 war against Iraq, President George Bush complained that the war protesters' drums kept him awake, but he would have been disturbed more if his bedroom had faced north. (Only a few Presidents, suspected to be particularly late sleepers, have chosen a bedroom facing north.)

Over the years some changes in White House facilities have been necessary in order to meet the special requirements or requests of the Presidents and their families. President Taft, who weighed over three hundred pounds, needed a super-sized bathtub installed for his private use. President Garfield's mother (the first to witness her own son's inauguration) required assistance in walking, and the first elevator in the White House was purchased

The Johnson family celebrated Christmas 1968 (their last in the White House) with a tree in the second-floor Oval Room.

for her. President Franklin Roosevelt, paralyzed from the waist down, later relied on the same elevator to move him from floor to floor and, fearful of fires, had the building inspected frequently. Fires in fireplaces were extinguished whenever he remained alone in a room—a marked contrast to President Nixon, who kept the fireplaces going even in summer because he liked the look of an open fire. Fortunately he could control the temperature by running an air conditioning system at the same time. By 1969, when Nixon became President, the White House's cooling system worked efficiently and well, a far cry from the primitive air conditioning hoses that had first been strung through the building in the hot summer of 1881 as President Garfield lay dying.

Because of its importance as the presidential residence, the White House is specially equipped to deal with any minor illness that occurs. In fact, its medical facilities come closer to that of a hospital than a home, and since the 1850s a doctor has usually been close at hand. President Buchanan was the first to invite a physician friend to live in the family quarters, and four decades later William McKinley was the first President to appoint an official White House physician, Surgeon General Presley Marion Rixey. Subsequent Presidents' families came to rely on a staff of military nurses and doctors to attend to minor illnesses, give vaccinations for foreign travel, and advise members of the household.

In the nineteenth century, taking a month or more off for recuperation was acceptable, but twentieth-century Presidents (as well as their wives) have been expected to get back to work quickly, even under difficult circumstances. President Reagan struggled to keep a partial schedule as soon as possible after the assassination attempt in March 1981, and after subsequent surgeries. Nancy Reagan and Betty Ford, who underwent mastectomies during their White House years, cited demands of their official duties as reasons for keeping their convalescences short.

The period following a death in the President's immediate family has always been a particularly difficult, trying time in the White House. The first occurrence was in 1800—thirty-year-old Charles Adams, son of John and Abigail Adams, died within days of his parents' move into the Executive Mansion. Abigail Adams had recently visited him in New York and she understood that he was an alcoholic and ill. But word of his death, although not entirely unexpected, rendered her and the President disconsolate for weeks. In 1862 President Lincoln's ten-year-old son Willie died of typhoid fever, and after his body was embalmed in the Green Room, Mary Lincoln vowed that she would never set foot in that room again. Sixty-two years later, Calvin Coolidge's younger son Calvin, Jr., contracted blood poisoning from a blister he got while playing tennis on the White House court, and within weeks the sixteen-year-old died.

Despite such enormous emotional strains, along with the pressure of presidential responsibilities, those who have lived in the White House find that something about the place pushes them on. Many of the Presidents and First Ladies have expressed a kind of awe at "living with history" and a desire to measure up to the legacy of their predecessors. Theodore Roosevelt was not easily impressed, but even he spoke of the effect those corridors had on him: he could almost see Lincoln (whose presence was strongest for T.R.) moving in and out of different rooms.

Others who have stayed at the White House, even for short visits, have encountered the mysterious "ghost" of the martyred President in the Lincoln Bedroom. Britain's Winston Churchill and Holland's Queen Juliana reported that they had glimpsed something strange. In 1987 Maureen Reagan, the President's daughter, who had slept in the Lincoln Bedroom with her husband Dennis Revell (six feet seven inches tall, he found the Lincoln bed the only one to his liking), admitted that they both had seen the "ghost." It was "an aura," she said, "sometimes red, sometimes orange" that appeared during the night. Even the Reagans' dog, Rex, seemed to sense something strange in that area and he would bark when he passed the Lincoln Bedroom but would refuse to enter.

Special tributes to famous predecessors can be daunting. Lyndon and Lady Bird Johnson, moving into the presidential bedroom, found two inscriptions on the mantel. One noted: "In this room Abraham Lincoln slept during his occupancy of the White House as President of the United States." The other, in small letters, read: "In this room lived John Fitzgerald Kennedy with his wife Jacqueline during the two years, ten months and two days he was President of the United States." Lady Bird Johnson concluded that this is one house where "history thunders down the corridor at you."

★★★

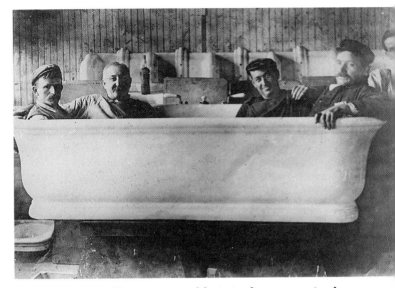

Four men could sit in the super-sized bathtub installed in the White House by President Taft (opposite page).

The Nixon family eats in the second-floor family
dining room. Counterclockwise: President Richard Nixon,
daughter Tricia, First Lady Pat Nixon, son-in-law David
Eisenhower, daughter Julie Eisenhower.

Regardless of their prominence in the nation's annals, all White House families have had to give some attention to paying the bills—a matter complicated by the fact that family and business have shared the same roof. George Washington set the precedent in rented quarters in New York City when he hired a chef and proceeded to pay out of his own pocket for the food consumed. More than two hundred years later that practice continues, although somewhat altered. The President's family pays for whatever it eats and uses—groceries, flowers, and laundry—but since the 1920s the government has picked up the bill for "official" guests.

More than one family has complained about the strain on its purse. Abigail Adams worried that she could not pay the food bills and remain solvent. William Henry Harrison, who was President for only one month, tried to control expenses by going out with a market basket and doing his own shopping. Calvin Coolidge went over the meat bills himself, and Mamie Eisenhower clipped coupons to get discounts. Some First Ladies attempted to cut costs by hiring professional caterers; others relied on their own employees to find ways to save.

In the original plan for the President's House, architect James Hoban located the kitchen in the middle of the ground floor on the north side of the building. Surrounding the kitchen were pantries and storage compartments for stocking provisions and storing pans, silver, china, and glasses. During two centuries the main kitchen has moved only once, to the northwest corner of the ground floor, and it has adapted well to the need to feed dozens of guests at some meals, hundreds of people at receptions, and the President's family every day.

A smaller kitchen alongside the main kitchen sufficed for occasions when the President's family dined alone, and several Presidents have installed their own experienced cooks to preside over that area. Sometimes different tastes within a family have necessitated two cooks. Franklin Roosevelt's preferences tended toward more sophisticated fare than his wife's housekeeper provided, and anyone looking over her menus will understand why—Henrietta Nesbitt's repertoire did not go beyond basic meat-and-potato dishes.

Eleanor Roosevelt had hired Mrs. Nesbitt, a Dutchess County, New York, neighbor, because she preferred "someone I know" in

A steward works in the pantry to prepare for a state dinner given by the Fords.

the job rather than a professional housekeeper. The First Lady, who took scant interest in food and probably would not have complained if served rice, potato, and cream sauce at the same meal, also approved of her housekeeper's dedication to economy. Mrs. Nesbitt once boasted that she served a meal to White House guests (who happened to be war veterans) for just over thirty cents per person.

The original White House kitchen, organized like that of a hotel or very large estate, featured two mammoth stone fireplaces and barred windows to let in natural light from the north. An annual coat of whitewash camouflaged greasy walls. Over decades, the kitchen changed to incorporate new technology. Electricity, installed in the White House in 1891, was the first step toward a fully electric kitchen by 1933. Further modernization added deep freezers, huge ranges, and all the trappings of the most demanding professional chef.

Being in the public eye, White House families must suffer the indignity of having even their food preferences scrutinized by the nation. Not all Presidents boasted the sophistication of Thomas Jef-

The White House family kitchen on the ground floor as it appeared in the 1890s.

ferson, whose wine cellar would have pleased a prince, or the polish of Chester Arthur, who brought his own French chef to the White House. Lyndon Johnson was known to make midnight refrigerator raids on the tapioca pudding and to object to beef-wrapped pâté as "spoiled meat"; Richard Nixon, although revealing himself to be a connoisseur of wine after leaving office, was known to pour catsup on his luncheon cottage cheese while he was President; and George Bush's veto on broccoli was broadcast beyond the White House kitchen to vegetable haters across the land.

Until 1961, the President's family had no dining room of its own on the second floor. Everyone had to come downstairs to eat in the private dining room on the state floor level or, as they would have in a hotel, request room service on a tray to be delivered upstairs. Housekeeper Henrietta Nesbitt's careful records during the 1930s show how frequently this latter option was exercised. Alongside every menu—carefully typed so that historians would know exactly what the Roosevelt family ate on any given day—Mrs. Nesbitt noted the number of people served. Sometimes, while two or three people might venture downstairs to the dining room, six others would ask for trays upstairs.

Jacqueline Kennedy objected to downstairs family meals and arranged for a smaller dining room on the second floor. The space she designated had already gone through several transformations. Once the bedroom of Theodore Roosevelt's daughter Alice, it had doubled as hospital when she had to have an appendectomy.

★ ★ ★

Alice Roosevelt Longworth's detailed accounts of the years she resided in the White House (including the story of her appendectomy and her confession that she used to go to the roof to smoke cigarettes) fascinated Americans. Eager to capture favorable public attention, many Presidents and their wives also provided interesting or amusing anecdotes for publication. The Grants, with their four attractive children and penchant for the public spotlight, permitted the press to quote their youngest son, Jesse, talking about his difficulties with dogs and with relatives. After daughter Nellie married in an extravagant celebration, and son Fred wed a Chicago socialite and then brought her to live at the White House, an entire nation seemed to want to read all the details—where everyone was sleeping and how the Grants' new granddaughter (weighing in at a

First Lady Nancy Reagan made a point of pretasting all dishes to be served to her guests.

The Carter family dines in the second-floor family dining room, its wallpaper restored after the previous family in residence, the Fords, substituted yellow painted walls. Clockwise from top: First Lady Rosalynn Carter; a family friend; daughter Amy; Lillian Carter, mother of the President; daughter-in-law Judy Langford Carter; son Chip; and granddaughter Sarah Rosemary Carter.

whopping twelve pounds at birth) was doing. First Lady Julia Grant obliged by doling out information as though she were a public relations agent.

Few White House families have included small children, and their rarity has increased the public's curiosity about them. Only Frances and Grover Cleveland, Edith and Theodore Roosevelt, and Jacqueline and John Kennedy had children less than five years old when they moved into the White House, although many others had young grandchildren. Caroline and John Kennedy, Jr., were the first young children of a President to live in the White House in more than fifty years, and photographers eagerly sought pictures of them whenever their mother permitted them to appear. Tourists inquired of White House guards where the baby slept and where Caroline's pony, Macaroni, was kept.

Growing up in the White House spotlight is not easy; public criticism can be loud and frequent. Franklin Roosevelt's granddaughter, Eleanor Dall Seagraves (Sistie), recalled as an adult that she had heard herself referred to as "that brat in the White House." Amy Carter was widely scolded for reading at the dinner table (as were her parents for permitting it).

Like typical grandparents, Presidents and First Ladies have been pleased whenever their young grandchildren have visited, and they have set aside parts of the lawn for them to play on. Despite criticism, Eleanor Roosevelt had an outdoor swing put up for grandchildren Sistie and Buzzie Dall after they came with their mother to live at the White House. Lyndon and Lady Bird Johnson, who had two grandchildren by the time they left office, created a tiny, secret garden for all young residents to enjoy.

Visits from grandchildren are singled out by staff as particularly pleasant times at the White House. During the difficult years following the Civil War, Andrew Johnson's wife, Eliza, made one of her very rare public appearances to attend a party honoring her grandchildren and their four hundred guests. One longtime White House employee, William Crook, observed that "there had never been a children's party so wonderful."

Ava Long, Head Housekeeper during the Hoover years, said that the only time she saw Lou Hoover in an exuberant mood was when her grandchildren came to stay with her. Their father began

The wallpaper in the second floor family dining room was removed during the Ford administration and the walls were painted yellow.

Eleanor Roosevelt encountered criticism when she decided to install a swing for her grandchildren Sistie and Buzzie Dall on the White House lawn.

In the early 1890s, President Benjamin Harrison's grandchildren became the most photographed children in the nation.

The number of Roosevelt grandchildren had grown by the time the President began a fourth term in 1945.

treatment for tuberculosis in December 1930, and while their mother attended to him, the three children, their nurse, and a governess moved into 1600 Pennsylvania Avenue. Ranging in age from Peggy (four and a half years) to Joan (eight months), the Hoover grandchildren remained half a year at the White House, and they could occasionally be seen with their grandparents greeting well-wishers from the South Portico steps.

White House residents worry about the safety of small children, and before each member of the household had security protection, every family took its own precautions. Frances Cleveland thought she could safely send her children and their nurse for a walk on the lawn until she observed the frightening result—strangers picking up her young daughter in admiration. Subsequently the First Lady insisted that the gates to the grounds be closed, and even when vicious rumors circulated about the children's physical and mental deficiencies, she refused to relent.

Julia Grant had objected earlier to the public's easy access to

the White House. "I closed those gates," she later wrote in her autobiography, and although there "was a public outcry against our exclusiveness, my children and I had a wonderful time."

Cameras had become popular by the 1890s and tourists stalked White House families, intent on getting their own personal snapshots. Benjamin Harrison's grandchildren could be seen on the lawn, pulled by their ponies or walked by their nurses, thus bringing a human touch to an otherwise distant President. Harrison's young grandson had his picture taken so many times that he became, according to some reports, the most photographed child in America. The child's fame grew until one southern congressman composed a verse about him, ending with the words: "Baby rules the White House / and damn it there you are."

Woodrow Wilson's first grandchild was born in the Executive Mansion in January 1915, but the baby failed to arouse the curiosity that had surrounded the Harrison grandchildren. A number of youngsters had moved through the White House in the intervening years, including the notoriously energetic and ingenious six children of Theodore Roosevelt. Journalist Jacob Riis, a good friend of T.R.'s, recalled seeing them slide down the banister to the state floor and parade their pet reptiles across the dining-room table. He was not present, however, for their most famous caper. When Archie Roosevelt became ill, his younger brother Quentin decided to comfort him by taking his favorite pony to the sickroom. The feat required coaxing the pony into the small White House elevator, but the visit cheered Archie and attracted considerable public attention. When a modern elevator was installed, the old one went on display at the Smithsonian Institution, mannequins of Quentin and the pony appropriately posed inside.

The Roosevelt boys sometimes intruded on their father's guests in very direct ways. John McIlhenny, a Rough Rider friend of the President's, was staying overnight at the White House and using a room separated from the Roosevelt boys' bathroom by a makeshift partition. Suddenly he got a wet sponge on top of his head.

Even the generally sedate daughters of President Wilson were tempted to mischief in the White House. They would join tourists walking through the mansion and then, without revealing their identity, make comments about the Wilson family—to the amuse-

President Woodrow Wilson, whose first grandson was born in the White House in January 1915, holds his first granddaughter, born later that same year.

President Theodore Roosevelt's son Quentin sits on the pony that later achieved fame for riding on the White House elevator.

Rosalynn and Amy Carter admire the White House garden.

This photograph of Abraham Lincoln and his son Tad in the White House appeared in *Harper's Weekly*, May 1865, just weeks after Lincoln's assassination.

ment of a few others who were in on the ruse and the shocked disbelief of those who were not.

If a President's children are of school age, several choices are available. Instruction can take place at one of the capital city's public schools (Amy Carter attended Thaddeus Stevens School) or one of the private academies (Luci Johnson enrolled at National Cathedral School). Presidential offspring can go away to boarding school or college, as the Coolidge sons did, or bring teachers in to start their own White House school class, as when the Kennedys arranged for a group of about twenty children to join daughter Caroline.

Abraham Lincoln's sons invited a few friends to share a tutor, and Julia Bayne, whose brothers went to the Lincoln White House school, implied that they all learned less than they could have and that Mary Lincoln, a particularly indulgent mother, went too far in her edict to "let the children have fun." The Garfield sons had their own tutor—Dr. Hawkes, who complained to the President that his charges talked too much and worked too little. The President reacted by saying he would check their assignments himself; the quality of their work immediately improved.

Choosing a school for one's children is usually no simple matter; the fishbowl nature of the White House ensures that it will be complicated. The security of the student must be considered and conditions assured for at least some scholarly progress. At the same time, most Presidents' families, aware that their White House years are limited, want to include children in as many of the special events and celebrations as possible. Almost as soon as Lyndon Johnson was inaugurated, Lady Bird began thinking of ways to persuade college-aged daughter Lynda to leave the University of Texas "and come back and live in Washington with us." The First Lady admitted to herself that this would be "no easy job."

A kind of camaraderie, reaching across generations and political party lines, develops among those with White House ties, and reunions occasionally occur. One such meeting in 1966 brought together members of seven Presidents' families to reminisce. Several of those present had actually lived in the White House—Mamie Eisenhower and her granddaughters, Franklin Roosevelt's son and granddaughter, and elderly Marthena Harrison Williams, who had caused a stir seventy-four years earlier when the White House was

put under quarantine while she recuperated from scarlet fever.

At another of these reunions, Margaret Truman joked that she was happy to meet her "fellow inmates," and President Taft's son Charles recounted how he had enlisted the help of young Quentin Roosevelt to plaster spitballs on all the White House paintings. The caper evidently inspired David Eisenhower, who admitted that on the last night he spent in the White House during his grandfather's second term he had put notes behind all the pictures, promising "I shall return"—and sure enough he did, as the son-in-law of President Nixon eight years later.

★★★

During their years in the White House, the President's family can turn to a variety of activities to fill any free time. If they choose to

Members of several Presidents' families posed at the White House for this photograph on November 28, 1966. Seated: (left to right) Julia Grant Cantacuzene, granddaughter of Ulysses Grant; Marthena Harrison Williams, granddaughter of Benjamin Harrison. Standing: (left to right) Eleanor Seagraves, granddaughter of Franklin Roosevelt; Mamie Eisenhower; Lady Bird Johnson; Lawrence Hoes, descendant of James Monroe; Mary and Barbara Ann Eisenhower, granddaughters of Dwight Eisenhower; Elliott Roosevelt, son of Franklin Roosevelt; Susan Eisenhower, granddaughter of Dwight Eisenhower; Barbara Eisenhower, daughter-in-law of Dwight Eisenhower; Mary Virginia Devine, great-granddaughter of Benjamin Harrison; John Roosevelt, son of Franklin Roosevelt; John Roosevelt's wife; and Helen Taft Manning, daughter of William Howard Taft.

read, there are plenty of books, at least since 1850 when Abigail Fillmore moved in and found that there were none. A former schoolteacher who had always liked having her own library, the First Lady persuaded Congress to appropriate two thousand dollars to buy volumes for the upstairs Oval Room. This collection was supplemented by additional purchases, and in the 1930s when the American Booksellers Association volunteered to donate reading matter, the library was relocated on the ground floor.

Presidential families need not leave the premises to view their favorite film or to take a class. In 1942 Franklin Roosevelt installed a movie theater in the East Colonnade, and it has provided relaxation for many Presidents. Jimmy Carter reportedly held the record for the most films watched there until he lost that distinction to Ronald Reagan (who sometimes preferred seeing films on a video in the upstairs family quarters). Bess Truman started a Spanish class for Washington wives and although Mamie Eisenhower, who enrolled, insisted that they learned little, the classes met regularly. Lady Bird Johnson called the White House "one big seminar," and Rosalynn Carter relied on experts to tutor her on many important national and international issues.

When Presidents and their families want recreation, the facilities are usually provided on the premises—at least they have been

For Christmas 1960 (their last in the White House), Dwight and Mamie Eisenhower invited relatives and friends to join them for a holiday meal.

The day after his inauguration, President George
Bush chatted with his mother, Dorothy Walker Bush,
in the Oval Office.

President Jimmy Carter enjoyed frequent tennis games on his own White House court.

during the twentieth century. John Quincy Adams had to take his morning swims in the Potomac (reportedly in the nude), but a hundred years later Franklin Roosevelt had the luxury of a pool. Limited by his paralysis, he had turned to swimming for exercise, and his doctors spoke publicly of how much he benefited from it. Schoolchildren from across the nation sent in their dimes and quarters to finance the construction of a White House pool, which was located in the colonnade connecting the West Wing to the residence. Roosevelt's four immediate successors enjoyed the pool, but Richard Nixon covered it up and converted the space to a pressroom. During Gerald Ford's presidency, funds were obtained from private sources to build another pool on the South Lawn.

Harry Truman turned to other types of recreation—poker or bowling—and had an alley installed in the West Wing. More than twenty years later Pat Nixon would go to relax in another bowling alley on the ground floor of the White House, near the area where Edith Wilson had once learned to ride a bicycle.

Among the top White House "perks" is a private tennis court, complete with courtside table and soft drinks. When President Bush, who interspersed jogging with horseshoes in his recreation program, put son Marvin in charge of allocating playing time, someone joked that he had captured "one of the most powerful jobs in the new administration."

The new outdoor swimming pool, built with private donations, served President Ford as the setting for a press conference.

For other leisure moments there are pets, and the White House has sheltered an incredible variety of animal life in two hundred years, rivaling a zoological park in its array of rabbits, snakes, turtles, and tropical fish. In 1969 Margaret Truman published an entire book on the subject, *White House Pets*.

The tradition of keeping animals at the White House began when Thomas Jefferson had cages built on the White House lawn for bears brought back from the Western journey of Lewis and Clark. Forty years later, the first American expedition to Japan returned with many souvenirs, including some tiny "sleeve dogs" for the President and his friends. The minute dogs resembled birds, and one observer noted that "a coffee saucer made ample scampering ground."

Personal pets often have to be cared for by the White House staff who, when the job becomes too burdensome, find ways of cutting back. The Grants' young son Jesse acquired several dogs, but one after another they died. Finally the President announced that the entire staff would be fired if another dog died, and the next one survived the remainder of Grant's presidency.

President Hoover (second from left) joined aides and reporters for thirty minutes of medicine ball each morning at seven before beginning work.

First Lady Grace Coolidge, famous for her fondness for animals, is shown with her raccoon Rebecca.

President and Mrs. Ford and their daughter Susan pose with Liberty and her first litter of puppies.

President Bush relaxes with the family dog, Millie.

The names of many of the dogs belonging to the Presidents and their families have become household words. Millions of Americans came to recognize Warren Harding's airedale, Laddie Boy, and Lyndon Johnson's beagles, Him and Her. Franklin Roosevelt's Scotty Fala and the Fords' golden retriever Liberty became familiar White House figures, and television viewers often saw First Lady Nancy Reagan trailing at the leash of her dog Rex after she stepped out of the presidential helicopter onto the South Lawn. Barbara Bush endeared herself to millions of animal lovers when, almost as soon as she had moved into the White House, she provided a birthing room for the family dog, Millie (the same area that had once been used by Nancy Reagan as a hair salon). In 1990 *Millie's Book* appeared in print, the first autobiography of a presidential pet.

★★★

President Roosevelt's dog Fala became a favorite of the nation and was frequently photographed alongside the President.

President Johnson's grandson Patrick Lyndon Nugent (center) celebrates his first birthday with a White House party in June 1968.

Every family marks some milestones of its own—wedding anniversaries, birthdays, marriages of sons and daughters—and the First Family is no exception. Some have struggled to keep these observances private, drawing a firm line between themselves and the world, while others have willingly transformed these dates into public celebrations. Nineteenth century Presidents, in particular, scheduled large parties to observe personal milestones, but that practice gradually became less popular. The Hoovers were noted for having many dinner guests throughout the year, but on their wedding anniversary they dined alone. The Franklin Roosevelts paid little attention to special days—at least for adults—and housekeeper Henrietta Nesbitt's records show only a cryptic notation: "birthday cake" on the menu.

Children's birthday parties in the White House illustrate once again how its public and private roles merge. Franklin Roosevelt's grandchildren had their celebrations arranged by the First Lady's secretary, who carefully preserved the records which can now be found in the Library of Congress. Edith Helm, who worked for several Presidents' wives, noted the names of young friends of Sistie Dall who agreed to attend her party on March 24, 1934, and those who declined—almost as though this were a state dinner or important political event. The invitation to Sistie's party came in two sections—one a typical juvenile card and the other featuring the presidential seal. Like so many other things in the Roosevelt White House during the years of the Great Depression, the invitations show a touch of frugality. They were evidently ordered in bulk, and the same one (with the day and hour changed) sufficed for several different occasions.

While in residence at the White House, Presidents' families find it hard to ignore the public's curiosity; gifts exchanged among themselves become part of the national record. The Reagans dutifully listed for the press the practical items they presented each other—often riding gear or ranch equipment for their California retreat.

Gifts from outside the family are another matter. Congress sets a limit on the value of items that a Chief Executive may accept, and the limit applies to his spouse and children as well as to himself. Items worth more than a designated amount become public property, to be turned over to a museum or left for the nation's use.

But such restrictions are recent, as a look through presidential papers shows. Lou Hoover hesitated to take a new Cadillac but then accepted in a note appropriate to this woman who loved horseback riding: "We decline most of the commercial gifts offered us," she wrote the donor, but "this Cadillac seems so much like a new colt just come in from the pasture that we cannot resist adding her to our Cadillac stable."

When gifts were offered to celebrate a personal event such as a wedding anniversary, lines between personal friends and business associates merged in uncomfortable ways. Helen and William Howard Taft celebrated their twenty-fifth anniversary with a huge party on the South Lawn of the White House in June 1911. Thousands of invitations went out (the First Lady insisted that she kept no record of the exact number) and hundreds of costly gifts came in.

Young friends of Sistie Dall received this invitation to her White House birthday party.

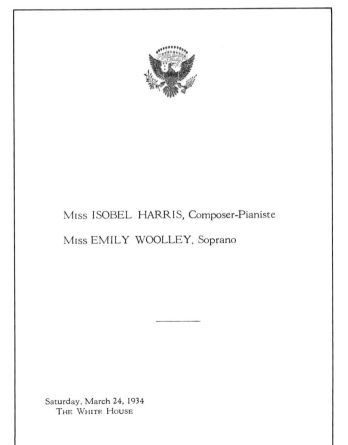

Miss ISOBEL HARRIS, Composer-Pianiste

Miss EMILY WOOLLEY, Soprano

Saturday, March 24, 1934
THE WHITE HOUSE

Helen Taft, the first President's wife to ride with her husband from the inauguration to the White House, caused even more comment when she held a large party at the Executive Mansion to celebrate her silver wedding anniversary.

One aide admitted, "I never knew there was so much silver in the world." One judge whom "the President hardly knows" sent a tureen two hundred years old costing eight thousand dollars. Embarrassed by the generosity and the appearance of impropriety, the President decreed that nothing should go on exhibit, but the First Lady stored all the gifts away with a later use in mind. She could erase the monograms on many pieces and pass them on as gifts to other people.

★★★

White House weddings, especially those that involve a member of a President's immediate family, are almost never entirely private affairs, as several brides have learned. The very first White House wedding almost escaped public attention—perhaps because its principals were President James Madison's widowed sister-in-law, Lucy Payne Washington, and Supreme Court Justice Thomas Todd. Even a bride could not upstage First Lady Dolley Madison, who reportedly "stole the show."

Within a decade, her successor Elizabeth Monroe upset Washingtonians by refusing to make her daughter's wedding a part of the capital's social season. Elizabeth Monroe insisted that the marriage of daughter Maria to her cousin, Samuel Gouverneur (who had served as the President's private secretary), be a strictly family affair. When the diplomatic community objected to the exclusion, the First Lady dispatched the Secretary of State to set them straight. Maria Monroe, the first daughter of a President to marry in the

White House, had her private "family" wedding in the first-floor Oval Room on Thursday evening March 9, 1820, and then five days later a reception was held for the newlyweds in the East Room.

While such small, relatively private ceremonies would continue to dot White House history (President Tyler's daughter married in a quiet ceremony in January 1842), larger, more public celebrations became common in the late nineteenth century. In 1874 President Grant's only daughter Ellen (Nellie) wed Algernon Sartoris, whom she had met during a trip to Europe. At first the President objected —that Nellie, at eighteen years of age, was too young to wed—but then he relented and invited several hundred guests to what was later described as the "greatest social event" of Grant's presidency and "the most brilliant wedding in the history of the White House."

The East Room, newly redecorated in an ornate style characterized as "steamboat palace," was embellished further by numerous large flower arrangements. Orange blossoms were brought in

The East Room, in its rococo-revival style of the late 1800s, provided a festive party room.

Although she did not provide the press with photos of her wedding dress, Frances Folsom posed for this picture for her family.

from Florida, and one of those attending described the room as a "perfect bower of bloom." The Marine Band played as Nellie, attended by eight bridesmaids, made her way to a small, flower-covered platform to recite her vows.

For a while it seemed that Nellie Grant's marriage was the most interesting news story in the nation. Special newspaper supplements, printed with pictures and details of the ceremony, sold out as quickly as they could be printed. When the marriage failed a few years later, a national magazine, *Public Opinion,* noted that the entire nation was saddened because it "had assumed a half-way responsibility for the match."

If the wedding ceremony featured the Chief Executive as bridegroom, Americans showed even more interest. When Grover Cleveland married Frances Folsom on June 2, 1886, the guest list was considerably smaller than for the Grant wedding, but public interest for the first (and only) marriage of a President in the White House, was even greater.

The young bride (one month short of her twenty-second birthday) had just returned from Europe and so most of the arrangements were left to the President. A wedding in a bridegroom's home was hardly typical, but so many of the circumstances of this match went beyond the ordinary. The bride's grandfather, whose home might have served for the ceremony, had just died, and no one else in her family could provide a place that guaranteed the necessary privacy. The President, who belonged to no church, disliked the idea of being married in one. A hotel did not offer the desired setting nor could adequate security and privacy be guaranteed there. Almost by default, the White House was chosen, and the President himself penned the invitations to cabinet members and a few close friends, about twenty-eight in all.

Guests gathered in the Blue Room, and the Marine Band played Mendelssohn's "Wedding March." The bride and groom walked in together, took their vows, and then led their guests to the State Dining Room where everyone feasted on a twenty-pound salmon (one of the largest ever recorded as coming from the Connecticut River) and tasted the four-tiered wedding cake that had been baked in New York. The man responsible for transporting the cake to Washington had taken the overnight train and had gone

When the Clevelands barred the press from covering the wedding ceremony, *Harper's Weekly* published its own version.

without sleep in order to make sure the cake arrived in perfect condition.

Many years later a Washington woman recalled how she had been only ten years old at the time of President Cleveland's marriage and that she and her young friends had stood with noses pressed against the White House fence to see as much as they could. Although she never had a glimpse of the bride and groom, she had heard the Marine Band and had seen "the huge banks of flowers and ferns in the windows."

Journalists went wild. Many camped on the White House lawn and others tried to hide among the catering staff and musicians. Barred from the mansion for the ceremony, reporters simply made up their own versions of what happened. The President had insisted that he wanted none of the sentimental trappings typically

After her marriage to Nicholas Longworth,
Alice Roosevelt posed with him and her father,
President Theodore Roosevelt (right).

associated with weddings, such as horseshoes and flower arrangements in the shape of wedding bells, but one national magazine printed a picture of him and his bride standing under both a horseshoe and a wedding bell. When the couple left for a honeymoon in nearby Maryland, reporters dogged their steps, hid in the shrubbery surrounding the honeymoon cottage, and took photographs whenever the Clevelands emerged for some fresh air.

Edith Roosevelt hoped to avoid some of this circus setting when her stepdaughter, Alice, married Nicholas Longworth, a prominent Republican congressman, on February 17, 1906. Arrangements were not simple, since a thousand guests were invited, and three separate entrances were designated for their use. The East Room had just been redecorated in 1902, and Nellie Grant Sartoris (who was a guest at the Roosevelt wedding) must have been struck by the contrast between this wedding and her own. Only a few tasteful flower arrangements adorned the room, and the bride, without any attendants, walked with her father to an improvised altar. The bride's stepmother had benefited from the Clevelands' experience with the press, and the First Lady permitted photographs of the bride's dress to be distributed. But in spite of all her cooperation, errors in journalism did creep in. Reports that the wedding party paraded down the big White House staircase were unfounded. Edith Roosevelt said, "We descended in the elevator."

Details of Alice Roosevelt's wedding became part of the White House social record and a model for others that followed. When two of Woodrow and Ellen Wilson's daughters decided on White House weddings, the staff looked to the Roosevelt nuptials for hints on arrangements. The first to wed, Jessie, chose Tuesday November 25, 1913, a day that turned out to be mild for late autumn. Invited guests (including military officers, foreign diplomats, cabinet members, relatives, and family friends) were told to present their admission tickets at the White House gates.

The bridegroom, Francis (Frank) Sayre, had an uncomfortable moment when he arrived for the ceremony and realized that he had neither a ticket nor any identification documents. He had been out walking on the Virginia shore with a friend that day and had come directly to the White House, where he found unusually tight security arrangements. When a guard asked who he was, Sayre recalled, "I told him I was the bridegroom but he replied that anyone could

President Wilson's youngest daughter married in a small White House ceremony in May 1914.

claim to be the groom. I suggested he call the Captain, because if I did not get inside there would be no wedding."

As in the two previous East Room weddings, Frank Sayre and Jessie Wilson took their vows in front of a low dais set up near the long outside wall, and the Marine Band played. Guests filed through the Blue Room, had refreshments in the State Dining Room, and then returned to the East Room, where the carpets were rolled back for dancing.

The bridegroom recalled that he and Jessie had a "tricky time getting away." Rumor had it that newsmen were vying for the best story about the couple's wedding trip plans, and a one-thousand-dollar reward awaited the winner. Frank and Jessie enlisted the help of a friend who let them use his car rather than a more recognizable White House vehicle, and a Secret Service man on a motorcycle cooperated by tying up traffic while they escaped. Then, after crossing over into Virginia, the newlyweds exchanged the first car for another one (equally inconspicuous) and, on their way to Baltimore, drove back past an unsuspecting crowd gathered outside the White House.

When President Wilson's youngest daughter, Eleanor (Nellie), married William Gibbs McAdoo six months later, circumstances made a smaller ceremony appropriate. The bridegroom was widowed and the bride's mother was ill with Bright's disease, which would prove fatal three months later, so only eighty guests were invited for the 6 P.M. ceremony in the Blue Room. This time the ruse to outwit reporters went a little differently. The bridegroom arranged for several White House cars and his own personal automobile to be parked conspicuously in different places. Then, after the ceremony, McAdoo enlisted the help of several guests; pretending to be the bridal party, they ran to the various cars and sped away, thus confusing reporters and dividing their attention while the real newlyweds escaped in another automobile that had been hidden behind some bushes.

A hiatus occurred in White House weddings—at least for Presidents' daughters—until the 1960s, when there were three. Luci Johnson, dubbed the "first White House bride" in fifty-two years, did not actually marry in the Executive Mansion. She had converted to Catholicism and her wedding mass was celebrated on August 6, 1966, at the Shrine of Immaculate Conception. But just about every

At the White House reception following Luci Johnson's marriage to Patrick Nugent, guests feasted on an enormous seven-tiered cake.

other element of the festivities took place at 1600 Pennsylvania Avenue: intricate planning, photography, and reception.

Since curiosity was at such a peak, newspapers wanted to publish a picture of the bridal gown before the wedding, but Luci was superstitious (or romantic) enough to want the bridegroom, Patrick Nugent, to see it for the first time when she wore it to the altar. Great effort went into helping her keep the secret. J. B. West, Chief Usher, noted that the white gown was locked in the Lincoln Bedroom, and no one was permitted to enter. When Luci decided she wanted to be photographed in the dress in the East Room, the entire White House had to be declared off-limits until she accomplished her mission. For an hour and a half no one, not even the housecleaners, walked through the White House corridors. Chief

Lynda Bird Johnson descends the main staircase
on the arm of her father for her marriage in the
East Room, December 9, 1967.

Usher West recalled that there was "tighter security than there had been during the Cuban missile crisis."

On the day of the wedding, the Executive Mansion was transformed. The upstairs hall was screened off into a beauty shop so bridesmaids could get their hair and makeup done by experts. Downstairs the state rooms were beautifully decorated and all set for the reception. After the ceremony, on a day Lady Bird described as the hottest of the summer, guests returned to the air-conditioned White House where a receiving line formed to greet them in the Blue Room. Then everyone filed into the East Room to watch the President's daughter cut the seven-tiered wedding cake.

On this one occasion, the White House staff proved overly efficient. When the bride prepared to change into her going-away outfit, she found that it had already been packed and taken away. Her mother admitted to having some nervous moments until the outfit was found and brought back.

Luci's older sister, Lynda, married on a crisp day in December 1967, and she chose a White House ceremony for her wedding to Charles Robb (whom she had met when he served as a military aide at the White House). Lynda's wedding followed the model set by Alice Roosevelt—with the ceremony in the East Room—but, unlike Alice and her father, Lynda and her father really did descend the famous stairway.

Julie Nixon, whose marriage to David Eisenhower, grandson of the former President, was scheduled to occur one month before her parents moved into the White House, chose another site—a New York church—but two years later her sister Tricia decided on a White House wedding when she married New York law student Edward F. Cox. Actually, the site was the Rose Garden, thus achieving a "first" for a President's daughter. Outdoor ceremonies are always risky in June, and no tent had been set up—in case of rain, the ceremony would have to be moved inside.

Julie Eisenhower recalled that the day of the wedding was gray with intermittent drizzle all through the morning. By about three o'clock, when guests began arriving for the 4 P.M. ceremony, no decision had yet been made to move inside. Julie and Tricia were "almost comically taking turns pacing in front of the beautiful arching window of the West Hall overlooking the Rose Garden." They could see the altar already set up under an iron gazebo covered with hundreds of white flowers. Military aides were trying to keep

President and Mrs. Nixon leave the Rose Garden after the marriage of their daughter Tricia in the first outdoor wedding of a President's daughter at the White House.

the guests' chairs dry, wiping them off and then preparing to carry them inside, only to change their minds and put them back in their previous places.

The President had retreated to a hideaway office across the street, and Pat Nixon left the final decision to the bride, who, in telephone conference with her father (who had conferred with the Air Force weather station), decided to rush the ceremony into a fifteen-minute storm clearing predicted for 4:30. The President escorted his daughter down the South Portico steps and along a path to the Rose Garden. The weather forecast proved accurate, and the ceremony was completed without rain. Then guests moved inside for dancing in the East Room. It was, Julie Eisenhower recalled, one of the first times her parents had danced in the White House.

Enormous publicity surrounded the Nixon-Cox wedding. Sixteen hundred reporters requested credentials and a separate tent was set up for them over the tennis court. As though to justify their presence, they published detailed, very personal information about the bride and groom, including her weight (ninety-eight pounds), her school record, and the fact that she collected Dresden and Meissen china. Exact wording of the vows went out on news wires. Besides biographical information on the bride and groom, press releases described the bandleader and told where he went to school, the ages of his three children, and his wife's first name. The bridegroom's souvenirs of the event—along with a piece of the wedding cake—went into the files at the Library of Congress, helping to document another White House family's records.

★★★

Few homes in America can match the White House as an elegant setting for a daughter's marriage or any other celebration. Nor can other private residences compete with it as a medical facility, travel agency, and communications network. Every family who lives there remarks on the advantages and the responsibilities of this once-in-a-lifetime opportunity. First-time visitors and long-time employees understand that the White House is, first and foremost, a residence for the President—a place for private moments, intimate family gatherings, and leisure activities with friends. In its first two centuries, the venerable mansion shared its fame with thirty-nine different families, and none of them would ever forget it.

After their daughter Tricia's Rose Garden wedding on June 12, 1971, President and Mrs. Nixon joined the bride and groom in a waltz in the East Room.

OFFICE OF THE PRESIDENT

In 1968 Lyndon Johnson announced from the Oval Office that he would not run for re-election.

★ When newspapers run headlines such as "The White House says . . ." or television reporters sign off "from the White House," they mean the office, not the residence. That small complex of offices, nestled in an extension on the west side of the mansion, looks more like the headquarters of a moderately successful corporation than the workplace for a world leader. From a modest, oval-shaped office, the Chief Executive presides over a staff that is spread out into the East Wing and fills two entire buildings nearby.

In some ways the President's office functions like a sizable city—apex of political power, center of a communications labyrinth, network of expert advisers and trusted staff. Even when a President leaves the

President George Bush, seated at a partners' desk in the Oval Office, speaks on one telephone while General Colin Powell uses another, during Operation Desert Storm, February 1991.

premises, the machinery and personnel continue to operate twenty-four hours a day, sifting reports, maintaining communications, and staying prepared to change course and implement new policy on a minute's notice. A score of telephone operators stand ready to put staff in contact with dozens of specialists familiar with the most obscure, distant parts of the world. The official phone directory of the Executive Office of the President lists more than four hundred people (although not all of them work in the White House complex), and that does not begin to cover the men and women, machines and operations that are considered part of the network.

When George Washington decided to combine residence and office under one roof he could hardly have anticipated the complex problems that twentieth century Presidents would confront—threats of terrorists and hostage-takers, international trade arrangements, and the demands of a nation of 240 million people. George Washington's staff was small—hardly larger than that needed by any gentleman who oversaw a sizable plantation, and most of his contemporaries employed relatives or friends, thus reinforcing the link between family and office.

The temptation to hire relatives was strengthened by the tradition that each President paid his secretaries from his own pocket. Not until 1857 did Congress approve an annual salary of $2,500 for an employee to handle secretarial duties. Even then, the custom of the President's office as a kind of multigeneration family club was so strong that James Buchanan, a bachelor with no sons of his own, employed his nephew James Buchanan Henry. Working for a relative, even one highly placed, had its drawbacks, and the young man, citing unreasonable demands by the President, quit after two years on the job.

Presidents forced to reach beyond relatives to find secretaries often brought them into the family circle and treated them like sons. Abraham Lincoln employed John Nicolay, a German-American from Illinois who had edited a small newspaper and worked for the fledgling Republican party in the 1860 election. Nicolay enlisted another young man from Illinois, John Hay, as his assistant, and the two were soon ensconced down the hall from where the Lincoln family slept.

For the President, "living above the shop" had its special problems as work and family matters overlapped and schedules merged into a seamless day that mixed children and business appointments, politics and pleasure. As long as the nation was small and the decisions few, the President worked at a leisurely pace and easily confined his office to part of the first floor. In the first administrations the few letters received each day at the White House could be piled on a single silver tray, opened at a small writing desk, and answered by a lone scribe or even by the recipient himself.

The first person to serve a full four-year term in the White

President Kennedy met with top advisers amidst scattered children's shoes.

George and Barbara Bush pose with Queen Elizabeth II
and Prince Philip in May 1991.

House, Thomas Jefferson, had eight years in which to organize his work space inside the mansion and get the office functioning efficiently. Unfortunately, he showed little administrative talent. Although he was a brilliant writer of memorable prose, Jefferson spoke poorly, without authority or clarity, and put little importance on office efficiency. Jumbled, irregular schedules often satisfy geniuses, and Jefferson's creative mind, which moved as easily from architecture to agronomy as it did from viticulture to vivisection, could thrive in a disorganized setting. Famous for announcing that he had no use for protocol at social events, Jefferson was just as casual about business, and the disorder that characterized seatings at his dinner table applied equally to his office.

The sunny, spacious room on the southwest corner of the White House that would later become the State Dining Room was Jefferson's choice for working, and one of his contemporaries described this "cabinet room" as holding a motley combination of furniture. In the center was a "long table, with drawers on each side" where the President kept his important papers alongside carpenter's tools and garden equipment. Maps lined the walls, and books, charts, and globes were interspersed with flowers and plants on the shelves. A mockingbird, Jefferson's "constant companion in his solitary and studious hours," remained in its cage while visitors were present, but when the President was left alone he would take the bird from the cage and permit it to fly around the room.

However informal Jefferson's office may have appeared, it did function as reception hall for the nation's leader, and it was here that representatives of other peoples came to call. The United States still commanded little attention from major European countries, but the North American Indians (as Native Americans were referred to at the time) already realized a need to make friendly gestures toward the President of the United States.

In 1804 a delegation of Osage Indians arrived at the President's House—the result of an invitation Jefferson had issued through Meriwether Lewis to come "at public expense." Their appearance and apparel intrigued Washingtonians, and one French artist profited from the curiosity by producing and selling crayon drawings of them.

Minor dignitaries from abroad also visited the President, often as much out of curiosity about this new American republic as out of a need to discuss matters of mutual interest. In 1805, when the

Osage delegation returned to Washington, their visit coincided with that of a Tunisian minister by the name of Meley Meley, who was traveling with his own large entourage. Accounts vary as to which of the two delegations appeared more exotic.

Meley's "numerous suite" came dressed in "Turkish costume, rich as silk, velvet, cashmere, gold and pearls could make it," while the "strangely contrasted" Osages wore deerskin moccasins and leggings, their faces and bodies painted. They must have made a colorful group as they sat down together at the President's table, where Jefferson surprised them by serving ice cream made from a recipe he had acquired during his stay in France. In the middle of a hot, humid Washington summer, the cold dessert caused no end of marveling and the President's guests carried away memories of an unforgettable dinner.

Of all the exotic foreigners who would visit the President's House during the next two centuries, none would arouse more curiosity than Marquis de Lafayette, whose assistance during the Revolution was still remembered by grateful Americans when he returned for a celebratory visit in 1824. The capital city still resembled a rough farming village in comparison to elegant European capitals, and one of Lafayette's aides expressed disbelief that the President of the United States would consent to reside in such unimposing surroundings. No important person in his own country would have received visitors in such a modest building.

American reporter Ann Royall also expressed her disappointment, describing the President's House as "unsavory," rendered more so by "a pack of the most insolent miscreants, in the character of his domestics, who guard the avenues to his presence."

None of this criticism could dampen Lafayette's welcome, and he found crowds everywhere eager to honor him, even putting his name on the top of ginger cakes. During that visit, he received the ultimate accolade: the park on the north side of the President's House was renamed to honor him.

As the United States grew and enhanced its importance in the world, a long line of distinguished foreign visitors made their way to the President's door. Skilled translators were not always available or present, especially in the nineteenth century, and there were many opportunities for misunderstanding. When a Chinese diplomatic

President Ford and Queen Elizabeth dance during the state dinner in honor of the Queen and Prince Philip at the White House, July 7, 1976.

On June 25, 1954, a meeting on the South Lawn
included Secretary of State John Foster Dulles,
British Prime Minister Winston Churchill,
President Dwight D. Eisenhower, and British Foreign
Secretary Anthony Eden.

President Rutherford B. Hayes greeted a delegation from China in the Blue Room, 1878.

delegation visited in 1878, dinner guests reported that they had to resort to childish mime. Royal guests could not be suitably accommodated overnight at the President's House, and in 1860 when the Prince of Wales visited, only he and two aides could sleep in the White House; the rest of his entourage stayed at the British Embassy.

The twentieth century saw an increase in foreign dignitaries and envoys, and by the 1940s Washington had become a virtual magnet for royalty and foreign heads of state. Eleanor Roosevelt wrote her daughter in some exasperation: "We've had the Dutch royal family for a night, all the Quezon family from the Philippines . . . and await the King of Greece . . . I forgot the President of Peru."

A visit by Winston Churchill during the Christmas season of 1941 turned out to be chaotic, and Eleanor Roosevelt remembered his stay as one of her most difficult times in the White House. The President's residence already carried an aura of being under siege —blackout curtains had gone up soon after the attack on Pearl Harbor—and the British Prime Minister arrived in some secrecy. An aide, a secretary, two Scotland Yard men, and a valet accompanied Churchill, and he expected all of them to be housed with him on the second floor of the White House.

Very quickly it became apparent that the British entourage expected to have considerable service and the run of the floor. They turned the Monroe Room (which the Roosevelts had used as a sitting room) into a map room and office, then proceeded to impose their own erratic schedules on an overworked domestic staff. Afternoon naps kept the Britons fresh, while the Roosevelts, who did not permit themselves the luxury of resting after lunch, tried to keep up the hectic pace. Even the energetic First Lady admitted that it always took several days to catch up on sleep after Churchill left.

At the conclusion of Mideast peace talks at Camp David in September 1978, President Jimmy Carter invited Egyptian President Anwar Sadat (seated on the left) and Israeli Prime Minister Menachem Begin back to the White House to sign the historic peace treaty.

Job seekers crowded the stairs on their way to the President's second floor office.

Almost from the day it was first occupied, the President's House hosted a steady stream of congressional representatives and office seekers (whose numbers grew along with the nation). After 1800, new states entered the Union in rapid succession, each one sending representatives and their families to the capital. Agencies and departments multiplied, and individuals came seeking jobs and favors for themselves, their relatives, and their friends.

Responding to the added responsibilities of the office, President Andrew Jackson began using part of the second floor for work, and John Tyler, upon taking office in 1841, ordered new desks equipped with cubbyholes and dividers. Andrew Jackson had used three rooms on the south side of the second floor, but the staffs of his successors claimed the entire east end.

Demands for the President's time were enormous. Each Chief Executive took responsibility for making hundreds of appointments, and job seekers descended on Washington after each presidential election to see the winner. Heading directly to the Executive Mansion, they congregated on the main floor and tried to take their case to the President or, failing that, to his closest assistant.

The stairway between the public first floor and the family-office second floor became famous and congested with traffic in both directions. Abraham Lincoln admitted to fleeing the residence just to avoid the crowds, and when he came down with a mild case of smallpox after delivering the Gettysburg Address he mused, "Now let the office seekers come for at last I have something I can give all of them."

After the Civil War ended in 1865, wealthy Southerners who had supported the rebellion against the Union flocked to Washington to ask for pardons. Their requests carried a certain urgency, since they were barred from political activity—including voting and holding office—until their mission was accomplished. President Andrew Johnson, a Tennesseean not unsympathetic to the Southern argument, thrived on the visible power his position gave him as men and women trooped up the White House steps to ask his forgiveness for themselves and members of their families.

Although Lincoln's wartime presidency left him little time for reorganizing the office, his successor—the tailor-turned-politician from Tennessee, Andrew Johnson—began to put some order into operations on the second floor. He permitted the installation of a telegraph in the mansion in 1866, thus beginning changes that would eventually turn that part of the White House into a maze of wires and cables necessary for communications. To accommodate a larger staff, Johnson put up partitions to make cubicles, and he installed file cabinets and additional desks. A receptionist sat in a room at the top of the stairs to sift out unnecessary intrusions.

Nineteenth-century Presidents maintained a private office of their own on the second floor, usually one of those rooms overlooking the large South Lawn. Ulysses S. Grant worked next door to the oval room where his children and wife would gather to talk and read. With a few steps he could move from a difficult political decision to relaxation with his family.

New inventions gradually made their way to the second floor of the White House, further complicating the split between its roles as home and office. The first telephone, installed in 1879 with the symbolic number "1," remained a single phone for three decades and it serves as a humble forebear of the hundreds of lines as-

Before a separate West Wing was built in 1902, the President's business callers went up a stairway located close to the north entrance, checked in with a receptionist, and then were ushered into one of the main offices.

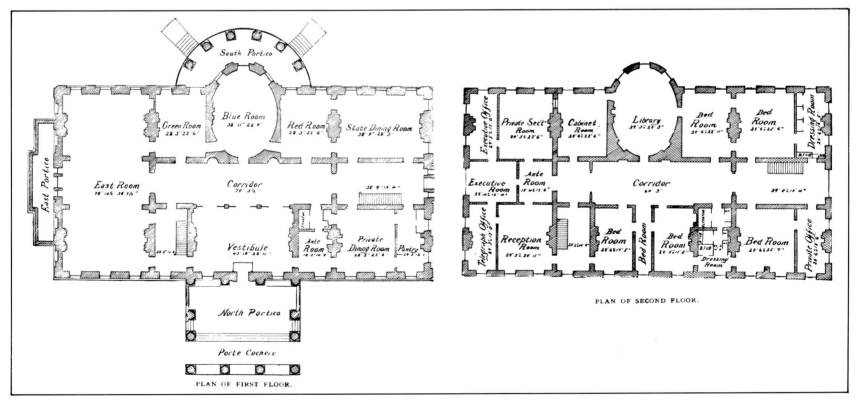

signed to the Executive Office a century later, when one month's telephone bill approached forty thousand dollars.

The typewriter was introduced into White House offices in 1880, bringing new noise levels with it and also, eventually, women workers who were needed to handle the ever increasing amounts of correspondence. Like most office staffs of the time, the President's remained entirely male until 1889 when Benjamin Harrison hired Alice B. Sanger as a stenographer. A veteran of Harrison's Indiana law office, she became the first woman to be employed in the White House in a job other than domestic service.

The increasing importance of the United States in the world—especially at the time of the Spanish-American War in 1898—helped keep the White House office growing. In 1900 Congress recognized the heavy workload and agreed to pay for two assistants and a "Secretary to the President." These staff members and their equipment cluttered much of the second floor, leaving President William McKinley and his wife Ida to confine their residence to cramped quarters in the west end.

In 1901 Theodore Roosevelt, McKinley's successor, felt compelled to make changes. Advisers, warning him that it was no longer safe to entertain crowds in the White House, suggested that whenever he anticipated large gatherings, he should arrange to have the floors reinforced with thick timbers. Earlier Presidents had

The President's staff, entirely male until 1889, worked in makeshift offices that also served as communications center, map room, and conference space.

A maze of wires cluttered the offices of the
presidential staff after the first telephone
was installed in 1879.

Before 1935, Presidents typically fled Washington for most of the summer, and this cartoon implies that Theodore Roosevelt took the White House with him to his Long Island estate.

used this safeguard at receptions for hundreds of guests, but now it would be routine for much smaller groups.

Theodore Roosevelt also faced the problem of finding enough seats for dinner guests. The President planned extensive entertaining, but the State Dining Room could accommodate no more than forty, and when he wished to host more, additional tables had to be set up in the large central hall or in the East Room—an unacceptable makeshift arrangement for a world leader.

Almost everyone agreed that the President's staff had outgrown the space they occupied on the second floor of the mansion, but no one wanted to ask the Roosevelt family to double up more than they had already done. Of course the President could have moved his family elsewhere, leaving the entire mansion for office space and official entertainment. But such an arrangement struck most Americans as wrong, and Theodore Roosevelt concurred in that view. When he was misquoted on the subject, he immediately set the record straight, saying: "Mrs. Roosevelt and I are firmly of the opinion that the President should live nowhere else than in the historic White House."

If the family stayed, then the question was where to build an office. Anything too close to the main house would impinge on its lines and mar its beauty; any sizable structure on the surrounding lawn would clutter and detract from the residence. The solution, described as "temporary" so as to disarm any critics, provided for an inconspicuous rectangular structure to the southwest of the White House, so close that the President could walk through a connecting colonnade and reach it in a few seconds.

The West Wing, as the office building became known, is traditionally off-limits to all but the President, his staff, and specially invited guests. Its heart is the Oval Office, the one room that more than any other has become synonymous with the presidency. An elliptical shape had not been part of the 1902 West Wing, but when the office building was enlarged in 1909 during William Howard Taft's administration, an Oval Office was designed. Rumors circulated that the shape derived from the President's rotund form—humorists joked that he had just lain down on the lawn while architects drew the outline of the room around him.

The real story behind the oval shape reaches back into Ameri-

One of the earliest photographs of the Blue Room in about 1867 shows use of the oval shape in floor coverings and ceiling decoration.

can history before there was a White House. President Washington followed the custom of his day by entertaining at levées—gatherings of men for conversation and refreshment in the late afternoon. Because his New York house could not accommodate sufficient seats, the President stood, and his guests typically formed a circle for conversation so that all participants appeared equal, with no one taking either the "head" or the "foot" of the room.

Eighteenth-century architectural styles promoted the idea of elliptical rooms. Bow windows were much in vogue in English Regency architecture around 1800, and President Washington

President Jimmy Carter's West Wing Oval Office.

showed a pronounced fondness for them. When the capital moved to Philadelphia and he rented the "largest house in town," the President included bow windows in his suggestions for remodeling. Washington may have communicated his preference to White House architect James Hoban, who designed an oval room on the south side of each floor.

With the oval shape so firmly entrenched in the history of the President's House, it is not surprising that architects echoed it in the West Wing. In delivering his design plans, Taft's architect, Nathan Wyeth, implied that its shape was no accident. "I have endeavored to show a dignified treatment," he wrote, "in keeping with the high purpose it is to serve." Although Franklin Roosevelt would later redesign the West Wing and put the Oval Office in the southeast corner, Taft's Oval Office was at the center, thus underlining the fact that it stood at the hub of operations.

Like all busy executives, Presidents retain space for several private studies and hideaways, one of the most convenient being a small suite just off the Oval Office. President Carter reportedly went there to work early in the morning, and occasionally he scheduled lunches there. In that same area President Bush put his personal computer and installed a private dining room.

After much of the office work was removed from the residence, an invitation to the second floor of the White House took on special cachet. In his first year as President, George Bush frequently invited congressmen and their spouses to visit the family quarters. He showed them the view from the "Truman balcony," snapped their photos in the Lincoln Bedroom, and walked them through bathrooms where they could observe the damp towels still on the floor. Such socializing might not change many votes but anyone who has wondered what the House looks like at the top of the stairs will understand that such visits cannot hurt.

★★★

Most twentieth century Presidents have divided their working time between the West Wing and the residence. Lyndon Johnson improvised conferences in many different rooms, and his Secretary of Defense, Clark Clifford, later wrote that he had learned of Johnson's decision not to seek reelection in 1968 when the President, still getting dressed for his televised speech to the nation, invited him into his bedroom to read the manuscript. Theodore Roosevelt used a room on the family floor for conferences, and his wife Edith jokingly said that the windows had to be opened frequently to "let out the politicians." Woodrow Wilson, who liked to type out his own letters and speeches, at least in a first draft, had his trusty portable typewriter transported many times from the Oval Office to his private study on the second floor. When the time came for signing the Underwood Tariff Act into law in 1913, Woodrow Wilson invited fifty of the law's backers to the Oval Office to witness his signature.

Such signature sessions had formerly been confined to the residence; the most famous one occurred on January 1, 1863, when Abraham Lincoln signed the Emancipation Proclamation. Turning to Secretary of State William Henry Seward, he explained that it was not uncertainty that caused him to dip his pen more than once before placing it on the paper: "I have been receiving calls and shaking hands since nine o'clock this morning till my arm is stiff and numb. Now this signature is one that will be closely examined. If they find my hand trembled, they will say 'He had some complications.'" Then Abraham Lincoln carefully signed his name.

So long as the office staff remained as small as that of Lincoln or of Wilson (the latter employed no more than forty), the West Wing's space sufficed, and even ceremonial events could be held there. As an example, in January 1915 Woodrow Wilson invited friends to witness the first transcontinental telephone call ever made from the Oval Office. What he did not know was that several staff members, eager to witness this unprecedented presidential communication, had arranged to eavesdrop on the call. They had placed an extension in the ushers' office just inside the north entrance to the residence and listened in awe as their President spoke with someone in San Francisco. Isabella Hagner, social secretary to First Lady Ellen Wilson, admitted that she had been one of those who had witnessed "this marvelous achievement."

After the death of his first wife in August 1914 and his remarriage in December 1915, Woodrow Wilson went less willingly to the Oval Office, preferring the privacy of the residence. Telephone and telegraph messages multiplied, especially after the entry of the United States into World War I in April 1917, and the increased number of clerks and employees required to keep the office functioning around the clock augmented the confusion. Wilson re-

In 1979 Jimmy and Rosalynn Carter welcomed Pope John Paul II to the White House, the first Pope to visit there.

treated to a study near the upstairs library where he kept his books. It was the only place, he wrote to a friend in May 1917, where "I can get things done."

Calvin Coolidge conducted most of his business in the West Wing, but by 1929 President Hoover found the space too small. Having come to the job from the business world, he was intent on efficiency and orderliness. The Republican nomination in 1928 was his first call to elective office, and he had little use for the kind of office management that most of his predecessors, schooled in the disarray of lesser political posts, took for granted.

President Gerald Ford talked with Japanese Emperor Hirohito in the Blue Room during a state dinner held in honor of the Emperor and the Empress Nagako, October 2, 1975.

President Hoover began by employing three private secretaries and about forty staff members, but that number quickly grew far too large to work in five small rooms on one floor of the West Wing. The building provided little opportunity for expansion. Low ceilings on the second floor reduced possibilities for its use as more than an attic, and the basement required further excavation before it could accommodate anything other than storage.

Staff members argued for expansion or even the more drastic alternative of transferring the President's office to a different location. But once again tradition proved inviolable, and the decision was made to hollow out additional rooms at the basement level.

The Director of Public Buildings, Ulysses S. Grant III (whose grandfather had once resided in the White House), took charge of the project. Excavation made space for a telegraph room, stenographers' and clerks' offices, locker rooms, and lounges on the lower level. Offices on the main floor were also redesigned so that the President's and his staff's offices were set off from the lobby and waiting rooms on the north.

By the summer of 1929 the West Wing was finished and functioning, but by year's end it required rebuilding again. Hoover's work space, so carefully renovated and enlarged, had caught fire and burned on Christmas Eve. The Hoovers were inside the residence that evening, enjoying a holiday dinner with family and friends, when an employee came to inform them of the flames coming out of the office building.

Guests in dinner jackets pitched in to help rescue files, and the President, who stayed on the west terrace to direct the action, reminded them that a small dog had been locked in the building that night so as to be given as a surprise to a child on Christmas morning. In an ironic twist, the President who would soon earn his countrymen's wrath for appearing insensitive to their economic plight remembered to order the dog's rescue.

In spite of the help offered from volunteers and the city's fire fighters, the building burned, except for some skeletal walls and partitions. Coming so soon after the debacle on Wall Street in October 1929, this did not seem a propitious time for talk about new construction; and accounts of the rebuilding disguised it as "general repairs." This was a ruse that had worked after the 1814 burn-

As part of their official duties President and Mrs. Kennedy prepare to meet guests at a State Dinner in honor of the Grand Duchess of Luxembourg.

President Herbert Hoover addressed a crowd gathered on the lawn outside his Office.

ing of the White House by the British and it would be used again when the residence was gutted and restored in the 1940s.

As soon as the work was finished, Hoover's large staff quickly made use of all the increased space, setting new records for the number of communications sent and received. In 1930, the first full year of the Hoover presidency, 77,055 telephone calls originated in the West Wing and nearly five times that number were received. The staff had to commandeer space in rooms that connected the main building to the West Wing, and in the process they pushed domestic services, such as laundry, into other areas.

The Great Depression crippled Hoover's presidency and limited him to one term, paving the way for Franklin Roosevelt to take office in the bleakest days of the economic downturn. Roosevelt's physical disability, resulting from poliomyelitis (infantile paralysis) twelve years earlier, made the trip to the Oval Office difficult (although he later used the elevator and an armless wheelchair with great ease) and for his first few days as President he worked in the residence.

Just hours after his own inauguration, Roosevelt summoned his cabinet members for a meeting. The Hoovers had just vacated the White House, leaving the upstairs Oval Room furnished with only a few chairs, a sofa, and a bare desk. Frances Perkins, assuming her title of Secretary of Labor—the first woman to hold cabinet rank— noted that "it never looked so tidy again as it did that night."

Roosevelt would continue to use the Oval Room for ceremonial parts of his job and for entertaining. He signed the Emergency Banking Act of 1933 and held some of his press conferences in that room, but he also liked to intersperse socializing with business, mixing drinks for colleagues or inviting them to join him for a meal served on a tray there.

Roosevelt's first trip to the West Wing had its bad moments. His valet wheeled him over, assisted him onto a desk chair, and then left him alone—more alone than he would have liked, he later explained. The drawers had been emptied, all writing matter removed, and he could not even find a buzzer with which to summon help. Finally, the man just elected to pull the nation out of the worst depression in its history leaned back in his chair and shouted.

The next year, 1934, Roosevelt enlarged the West Wing and

President Franklin Roosevelt became famous for
delivering radio speeches from various rooms
in the White House.

President Kennedy made this style rocking chair famous, although his wife objected to its effect on her plan to restore the White House. "A rocking chair is a rocking chair," she said, "and there is not much you can do to cover it up."

reorganized his staff. A larger space was allocated to the Oval Office, now situated in the southeast corner where it looked out over the Rose Garden and occupied the same area that Ellen Wilson had once designated for drying laundry. When television viewers watch their Chief Executive deliver a speech from the Oval Office, it is this room, 36 feet long and 30 feet wide, that they are seeing.

Space is tight in the West Wing, which measures only about 60 by 90 feet. During Jimmy Carter's presidency, one employee estimated that each staff member assigned there got an average of about 70 square feet, although few would have relinquished that tiny space for larger quarters elsewhere. One Nixon aide explained the advantage of a basement cubicle within a few steps of the Oval Office: "Never underestimate the importance of proximity."

Even these modest dimensions had been achieved with some trepidation, and President Roosevelt carefully prepared public opinion to accept his expansion of the West Wing. In one of his Fireside Chats in June 1934, the President explained that he had no intention of impinging on the plans of the original designers, but his office required modernization. During the summer, while he went on an extended trip to the West Indies and Hawaii, work began to install "modern electric wiring and modern plumbing and modern means of keeping the offices cool in the hot Washington summers." The underground rooms would be expanded and a third floor of offices added. But the President assured his listeners that the "magnificent pattern" they all recognized would not be changed: "The artistic lines of the White House were the creation of master builders when our Republic was young. The simplicity and the strength of the structure remain in the face of every modern test."

Franklin Roosevelt was back working in the enlarged office building by December 4, bringing with him an executive staff that now numbered 120. But the stresses of the Great Depression, the multiplication of federal agencies, and World War II would soon render that number hopelessly inadequate. Bulletproof windows were installed in the Oval Office during World War II, and other changes were made to increase security, but the building's dimensions remained untouched.

Attempts to enlarge the West Wing during the Truman administration foundered, partly because of outrage at what seemed to be the desecration of a national monument. One cabinet member voiced his own objections in a letter to the President. He was concerned, he wrote, for the "thousands of people who came every day to see [the White House] as they would visit a shrine, not only because it houses the Chief Executive of the Nation but for what it represents in the hearts of the people."

Over the years each new administration has decorated the Oval Office to fit its own tastes. Colors change and paintings shift to reflect new heroes and hobbies. Americans who visit a presidential library such as that of Lyndon Johnson in Austin, Texas, or Jimmy Carter in Atlanta, Georgia, will understand how varied the same room can look. Each has a model of its namesake's Oval Office,

Caroline Kennedy (left) joins a friend under her father's Oval Office desk in June 1963.

and in comparison they seem like entirely different places.

Sometimes the changes are unplanned. In an ironic twist, Lyndon Johnson moved into a freshly decorated Oval Office immediately after the Kennedy assassination. Jacqueline Kennedy had chosen the red carpet weeks earlier, but the installation had been delayed because of an air-conditioning problem. Just as the carpet was finally being installed, word came from Dallas that President Kennedy had been shot. Work continued—but for a different occupant.

Lyndon Johnson replaced Kennedy's famous rocking chair with one of his own and substituted family photos for the naval paintings and watercolors that had pleased his predecessor. A larger, simpler desk replaced the famous "Resolute" desk, a favorite of many Presidents and the one that doubled as play space for the Kennedy children when they visited their father in his office.

The "Resolute" desk first came into the White House in 1880 when the British government sent it to President Rutherford B. Hayes as a symbol of amicable relations between their two nations. Timber used to make the desk had come from the oak of a British ship, the HMS *Resolute,* abandoned in the Arctic in 1854 and then rescued for the Britons by American whalers.

Whether a President chooses to use this desk or another one, to have the presidential seal woven in the middle of the rug or not, to make the walls blue or yellow, is up to him, but virtually no President leaves the room unchanged. Each occupant tries to underplay the cost of redecoration. President Ford had his wife's press secretary issue a tiny announcement in November 1974 that he would be furnishing the Oval Office to reflect his own taste and provide a "warmer feeling" than that in President Nixon's office. The carefully phrased announcement left the impression that the cost would be negligible since most of the furniture would come from storerooms and other parts of the White House collection.

Even successive Presidents of the same political party customize the Oval Office furnishings to their own liking. Ronald Reagan installed a wooden floor of Kentucky oak and walnut (in place of the "wood-appearing" vinyl that had been there since 1969) and covered it with a salmon colored rug featuring the presidential seal. President Bush chose a moderate-size partners' desk (so-called be-

John F. Kennedy used the "Resolute" desk, given to President Rutherford B. Hayes by the British in 1880.

President Reagan looks over papers in the Oval Office, decorated during his tenure with Western art, including the sculptures in the background.

cause drawers on both sides permit two people to work there simultaneously) and a large blue rug featuring the presidential seal prominently in the center.

Although the Oval Office has remained central (symbolically, if not physically) to the West Wing since 1909, assignment of the space around it has shifted. As in any business operation, the size of one's office helps signal status. Even the waiting room (how big it is and whether every caller is treated the same) conveys a message about how the President does business, and the press and political insiders scrutinize the assignments made by each new administration. In 1985, as President Reagan began a second term by

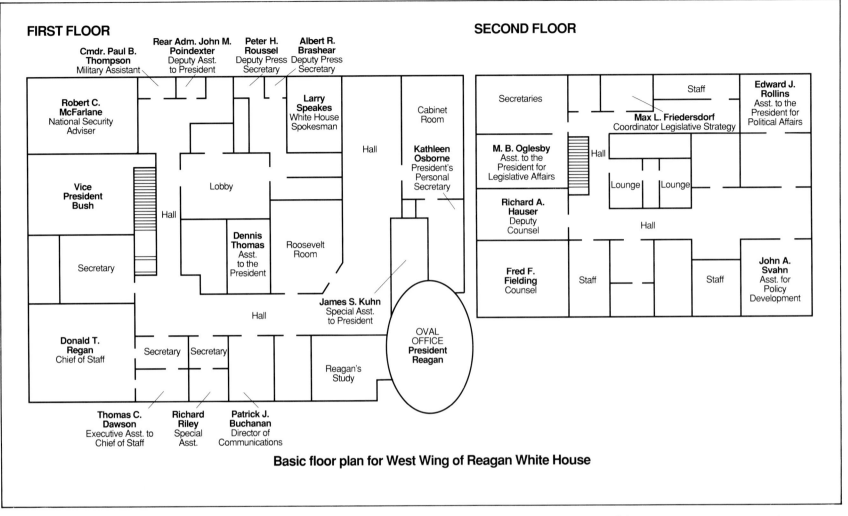

FIRST FLOOR

Cmdr. Paul B. Thompson — Military Assistant

Rear Adm. John M. Poindexter — Deputy Asst. to President

Peter H. Roussel — Deputy Press Secretary

Albert R. Brashear — Deputy Press Secretary

Robert C. McFarlane — National Security Adviser

Larry Speakes — White House Spokesman

Cabinet Room

Hall

Kathleen Osborne — President's Personal Secretary

Vice President Bush

Lobby

Hall

Secretary

Dennis Thomas — Asst. to the President

Roosevelt Room

James S. Kuhn — Special Asst. to President

Hall

OVAL OFFICE — President Reagan

Donald T. Regan — Chief of Staff

Secretary

Secretary

Reagan's Study

Thomas C. Dawson — Executive Asst. to Chief of Staff

Richard Riley — Special Asst.

Patrick J. Buchanan — Director of Communications

SECOND FLOOR

Secretaries

Staff

Max L. Friedersdorf — Coordinator Legislative Strategy

Edward J. Rollins — Asst. to the President for Political Affairs

M. B. Oglesby — Asst. to the President for Legislative Affairs

Hall

Lounge

Lounge

Richard A. Hauser — Deputy Counsel

Hall

Fred F. Fielding — Counsel

Staff

Staff

John A. Svahn — Asst. for Policy Development

Basic floor plan for West Wing of Reagan White House

shifting some of his top advisers and bringing in new people, a major newspaper provided a diagram of the West Wing. It showed the President's Chief of Staff, who oversees the entire operation of the Office of the President, ensconced in a large corner room that is closer to the Oval Office than is the Vice President's office. The National Security Adviser, Robert C. McFarlane, was using a first-floor office—he had previously been assigned basement quarters.

★ ★ ★

To an uninformed visitor, the West Wing's basement looks more like the underpinnings of a moderately successful corporation than the setting for decisions of world importance. Much of the space is set aside for services—a plaque on one door identifies it as a barbershop, a tiny 10-by-10-foot cubicle where Milton Pitts trimmed hair for President Nixon and then remained through three subsequent administrations. From across the corridor wafts the aroma of food from the staff's dining rooms. The paneled walls and blue fittings project a nautical feeling, hardly an accident since the Navy runs the dining hall and boat-loving Franklin Roosevelt oversaw its construction.

Staff dining (or "mess") privileges are among the most coveted perks of White House employment. The three small dining rooms can serve ninety people at one sitting, but even two shifts cannot accommodate all who claim the privilege. Family and friends of staff members beg to be included, and in 1979 one announcement of promotions implied that the biggest effect would be in the dining room—the new titles carried with them eligibility for eating in the White House mess.

Diligent control keeps many prospective diners out. A reporter for *The New Republic* learned that no journalists were allowed, and in January 1989, just as the Bush administration was settling in, Brent Scowcroft, the President's National Security Adviser, opened a meeting of the National Security Council staff by announcing that all matters were up for discussion except the "White House mess and parking privileges."

Within a few steps of the dining room is an inconspicuous area of special importance called the Situation Room, which is always staffed around the clock. Its origins date back to the failed Bay of Pigs invasion in 1961 when President Kennedy decided to convert this room, formerly used for storage and utilitarian plumbing, to a communications room for monitoring information affecting national security. Wherever he goes, the Chief Executive is always linked to this small room by complicated electronic equipment (commonly called the "football" and carried by a military aide). Information is relayed to the President within minutes of its being received. Next door to the Situation Room is a conference area, encased in a lead shield that can stymie the most sophisticated eavesdropping equipment.

In 1972 President Nixon had the Situation Room remodeled, and computer terminals, two safes, and wall-to-wall carpeting were installed so that it resembled thousands of offices across the country. One visitor described it as visually disappointing—with a dozen or so technicians going quietly about the work of monitoring video terminals, filing papers, and waiting for the moment when they would be expected to act quickly. Workers have been known to complain of boredom, but each knows that major change is always imminent. An almost infinite number of events at any spot in the world might require the President, through his National Security Adviser, to look to the people in this room for fast, accurate information on which to base a decision.

Especially in times of crisis, Presidents make frequent visits to the Situation Room. Lyndon Johnson went there often to monitor developments in Vietnam, and he was there in January 1968 when word came that the North Koreans had taken command of the American intelligence ship *Pueblo.* Information was crucial—the North Koreans charged that the Americans had violated the twelve-mile limit at sea, while the Americans insisted they had remained within international waters.

In contrast, Presidents rarely venture to the West Wing's second floor where low ceilings—a necessity if the building was to remain an inconspicuous adjunct to the large main structure—make the small offices appear cramped. Its leaky roof has become famous and resistant to change. As one spokesperson explained, no administration wants to undergo the disruption caused by a thorough repair, and each President leaves the leaks for a successor to plug up. On occasion, buckets have had to be strategically placed on the first floor to catch water that has leaked from the second floor.

Power radiates from the main floor of the West Wing where, in addition to the individual offices and the waiting room, two meeting rooms provide conference space. The first, which is centrally located, was dubbed the Fish Room by Franklin Roosevelt and decorated with memorabilia from his fishing trips. But in 1969 President Nixon renamed it the Roosevelt Room for his fellow Republican Theodore Roosevelt, who had presided over the original construction of the West Wing. Reporters noted a bipartisan nod, made possible by the room's exhibition of quotations from both Theodore and Franklin Roosevelt. But most of the room celebrates T.R.—his Nobel Prize, and his love of horses and the West.

The Roosevelt Room in the West Wing, used for small conferences and meetings, was called the Fish Room by President Franklin Roosevelt.

The other conference room, just a few steps away and facing out onto the Rose Garden, is known as the Cabinet Room, which should be familiar to every viewer of television news. The brown leather chairs surrounding the table are only temporary, and most of them are purchased by their respective occupants upon leaving the job. Each is marked with a small plaque identifying who sits there, and two of the chairs—belonging to the President and Vice-President—are distinguished from the others by their slightly higher backs. When he was President, Lyndon Johnson further enforced the notion of "having his own turf" by installing several buttons at

Until the Nixon administration, Presidents had no permanent studio for press conferences, and John Kennedy (here seated in his special rocking chair) sometimes used the Oval Office for interviews.

Flanked by Secretary of State Dean Rusk and
Secretary of Defense Robert McNamara in the Cabinet
Room, President Lyndon Johnson holds Courtney
Valenti, daughter of White House staffer Jack Valenti.

his place under the table—one of them a command for his favorite diet soft drink.

A few steps across the hall from the Cabinet Room, a Press Office underscores how much the Chief Executive's job has changed in two centuries. The first Presidents would not have understood the title or felt the need for a Press Secretary—someone to hand out news about what the President was doing and why. Twentieth-century Americans, however, came to know the names of several Press Secretaries better than those of the Vice Presidents: Pierre Salinger for Kennedy, Ron Ziegler for Nixon, Jody Powell for Carter, and Larry Speakes for Reagan.

The move toward having a separate spokesperson for the President began slowly. In the West Wing of 1902, Theodore Roosevelt allotted space for reporters next to his secretary's office. Journalists accustomed to hanging around the White House entrance, scrutinizing exits and entrances in hopes of scooping an important story, found themselves invited inside and thus acknowledged as a legitimate part of the governmental process. Reporters even merited their own telephones so they could phone their stories to the office rather than rely on a corps of young messengers to run back with the news.

Nothing so formal or organized as a press conference existed yet, although Theodore Roosevelt seemed to relish chats with individual reporters. Often these talks would occur while the President went about some other task such as reading and answering his mail. Oscar King Davis ("O.K." to his friends), a *New York Times* reporter, described how he would see the President two or three times a week, generally in the evening when Roosevelt came back to the office to clear up his desk before going to dress for dinner. Roosevelt "would glance over a letter, make an addition or alteration with his pen, and sign his name at the same time he was keeping up a steady fire of talk about whatever subject happened to be under discussion." This kind of exchange did not appeal to Woodrow Wilson, who, while still a political science professor, had recognized that he did better lecturing to large groups than talking with individual students in his office. Wilson invited reporters to come *en masse* to the Oval Office so he could set them straight on matters of public interest. More than one hundred showed up in March 1913, but the exchange did not go well. Edward Lowry, one of the reporters present that day, described how a few questions were asked, tentatively, and answered "crisply, politely, and in the fewest possible words. A pleasant time was not had by all."

Reluctant to abandon the idea of talking with reporters, Wilson scheduled another press conference a week later. When nearly two hundred correspondents appeared, the small Oval Office could not accommodate them and so the meeting adjourned to the East Room in the residence, thus setting a pattern that continues to this day for very important or celebratory press conferences.

Presidents following Wilson dealt with reporters in their own individual ways. Warren Harding, a newspaperman before going into politics, agreed to meet with them twice a week, and then he followed up this friendly overture by inviting them to play poker and referring to them genially as "our newspaper family." Even the taciturn Calvin Coolidge invited newspaper writers into his office, and Franklin Roosevelt thrived on the exchanges. As many as two hundred reporters would try to crowd around his desk which was, according to one observer, "covered with dolls, totems, and knick-knacks. It was like a meeting of a club."

Most Presidents preferred a little more distance between themselves and their interrogators, so they relied on a staff member whose job eventually got its own title, Press Secretary. The assignment had its special stresses—as an extreme example, two Press

Pierre Salinger, Press Secretary to President Kennedy, briefed reporters on White House decisions.

Secretaries serving Truman died on the job. Nevertheless, gradually Americans came to expect to hear much of the news about their President not from the man who held the office but from his Press Secretary.

In its attempt to distribute favorable reports about the President, the Press Office showers news organizations, fraternal associations, sports groups, and ethnic alliances with hundreds of press releases. So much activity requires a large staff, and in the 1980s one estimate placed the total number employed in presidential press activities at one hundred fifty—all of them under the direction of the Press Secretary, although not all working in the West Wing. Some had to be assigned space across the street in the Old Executive Office Building or in some more remote quarters.

This mushrooming growth in the President's Press Office had more than one explanation—the number of correspondents assigned to cover the President had also multiplied. In the early 1950s, television typically designated only fifteen minutes each day for national news, but by the 1980s several hours of programming went into people's homes every day. Correspondents assigned to cover the President had to fill up much of that time, and the White House "beat" became a popular one. Morning viewers came to expect their own favorite reporter on the screen at 7 A.M. talking directly "from the White House."

Since the West Wing predated the development of either radio or television, studio space for the Chief Executive was not provided, and Presidents struggled to make their own media arrangements. Calvin Coolidge gave the first radio speech by a Chief Executive in the White House, and First Lady Lou Hoover set up a tiny workplace on the second floor where she could practice with microphones before giving her talks on national radio.

Franklin Roosevelt, a natural master of radio communications, used the medium extensively, broadcasting from various rooms in the White House, including the Diplomatic Reception Room on the ground floor. He was bothered by the fact that his "Fireside Chats" were first staged in a room where there were no fireplaces. The one that had been there was covered up, and in 1941 the President had the fireplace restored, complete with mantel.

Roosevelt's successors continued to use the radio to address the nation, and Ronald Reagan scheduled weekly broadcasts on

Saturday mornings, but gradually Americans came to rely on television for news from their President. By 1969, ninety-five percent of American homes boasted at least one television set, and many had more. Lyndon Johnson understood the popularity of the medium—he had chafed at the limitation of seeing only one channel at a time and installed a giant console of three screens in the Oval Office so that he could watch three networks simultaneously.

Television cameras and the accompanying paraphernalia of teleprompters invaded every part of the White House. As the cameras became more maneuverable and required less light, almost any corner of the mansion was suitable. Nancy Reagan appeared in front of television cameras in the Map Room, and Barbara Bush scheduled interviews in the ground floor Library.

Presidents have sought a more permanent arrangement. John Kennedy experimented with answering reporters' questions in auditoriums outside the White House compound, but Lyndon Johnson wanted something more convenient. James Hagerty, who had served as Eisenhower's Press Secretary, came forward with a plan to turn the Fish Room, just steps from the Oval Office, into a full-time broadcast studio. If various branches of the media split the bill (estimated at a million dollars), the President could appear in front of cameras and be shown in homes across America several times a day. That project failed, but eventually Lyndon Johnson arranged for a makeshift studio to be set up in the White House theater so that he could rehearse his remarks before delivering them to the press.

Johnson also courted the press by improving their workplace. The Fourth Estate's status in the West Wing had not improved much since the days when Theodore Roosevelt permitted the press to wait in the lobby rather than outside. The lobby provided few amenities, and it resembled the waiting room of a train station more than part of the Executive Office. Coats and discarded paper cups piled up on the center table as reporters lounged around, waiting for a story worth writing. Johnson had the lobby refurbished and provided more seating. The table was removed and a portrait of George Washington hung over the receptionist's desk as a reminder of the dignity of the office.

When Richard Nixon visited reporters one Sunday in 1969, he found their quarters cramped and unattractive, and he inquired with some disdain of one reporter present, "Is this where you

President Lyndon Johnson's Oval Office included a triple-screen television console.

work?" The result was a completely new facility, in the space where Franklin Roosevelt's swimming pool had once been—in the colonnade connecting the office wing to the residence.

Finally, reporters had their own turf—a lounge equipped with telephones and individual radio booths, seats for listening to the President or one of his spokespeople, a raised platform for cameras, and a podium with its own blue curtain and White House logo. At the rear of this low-ceilinged room is a hodgepodge of Formica-topped tables, making the space seem more like part of a thriving newspaper than part of the President's office. Seats can accommodate sixty to seventy reporters, but the room expands for an unknown number of standees when a big story breaks. On a typical day when the President is at work, twenty or so reporters might wait at any one time for a story, but on a Saturday or a quiet summer day, when the President is out of town, the area is deserted, with only a cleaning crew and perhaps one late-filing reporter on the premises.

Some journalists caviled that the Press Room gave them a less advantageous point from which to see who was entering the President's office—their former quarters had provided more proximity—but they remained downstairs. Additional remodeling in 1981 pushed amenities back, as lounging chairs and coffee machines gave way to more work areas. The Reagan administration assigned permanent seats in the Press Room for each network or major newspaper so that the President could more easily recognize individuals and call them by name.

Television correspondents like to deliver their remarks from outside the Oval Office so that the West Wing forms a graceful, low backdrop. Tourists and other visitors learn to recognize the reporters, each of them outfitted with a microphone and trailed by cameras and wires necessary to transmit their observations across the continent and around the world.

In spite of the efficient organization of the West Wing offices, the White House residence continues to offer some very obvious advantages for Presidents to work. The mansion's size and multiple entries conceal entrances and exits. An adviser or covert messenger can make an appearance without alerting the press, and the President can be awakened during the night or interrupted at lunch for a decision or a briefing.

Jody Powell, Press Secretary to President Carter, spoke with journalists in the Press Briefing Room.

During World War II, President Roosevelt set up a Map Room on the ground floor of the residence and limited access to a very few people. It served as a communications center for vital information related to the war, including the movement and progress of Army and Navy units. President William McKinley had followed naval maneuvers during the Spanish-American War in a map room that he improvised on the second floor of the residence, but Roosevelt was probably more impressed by the example of Winston Churchill who designated one room in his underground London bunker as a map room.

In the White House version, large wall maps with different-colored pins marking positions and progress of troops appealed to President Roosevelt. He did request one personal favor, though, quite outside normal operations: One pin marked the ship on which his son was serving in the Pacific. It was the first pin the President looked for whenever he entered the room.

Roosevelt's Map Room served more than cartography purposes. Secret communications came in for decoding, and the President's messages went out. A dozen men, equally divided between Army and Navy, filed materials and maneuvered the map pins to reflect the latest intelligence. Because it was considered a military facility, the Map Room was off-limits to all but the President and a half dozen of his most trusted advisers. Even his cabinet members, his Secret Service guards, and his family were barred. Doors to the room were either sealed off (as to the adjoining Diplomatic Reception Room) or guarded around the clock by a White House policeman.

Only the energetic First Lady, Eleanor Roosevelt, seems to have breached the security precautions, rushing past an amazed guard one day in order to learn the whereabouts of one of her sons in combat. She even took Madame Chiang Kai-shek, wife of the Chinese Nationalist leader, on a tour of the room, but this time the staff had some warning, and they scrambled the map pins and rearranged the room before the women arrived.

Although security precautions require very limited access to parts of the White House, the President seeks to appear open to constituents' comments and criticisms, even maintaining a listed phone number. In addition to the regular switchboard, there is another manned by the military, and this is the one that takes care of the President's communications when he is traveling. Exceptions are sometimes made, though, as when Lyndon Johnson objected to the male voice of a Signal Corps officer asking "Number, please" and ordered a female White House operator to go along to handle calls.

For White House telephoning, President Johnson relied on a crew of twenty operators—actually he relied on them a lot because he broke all records in using the telephone to confer with advisers and to cajole congressmen into taking a particular position or casting a needed vote. The operators, justly fabled as able to find anyone, anywhere, work in shifts around the clock. Because they typically stay from one administration to the next, they develop enormous expertise and compile large files of unlisted, hard-to-find numbers that they closely guard and rarely share. Even Jimmy

The Map Room, used as a situation room during World War II, now serves as a meeting room.

Nancy Reagan met with media advisers in the Map
Room on the ground floor of the residence.

111

Carter, after leaving the White House, was refused when he requested numbers from the operators' files, but he did get an offer of personal help whenever he wanted to place a call.

One of the most famous stories about the White House switchboard concerns the Kennedy years. The President decided to test the skill of the operator on duty by requesting the whereabouts of a man who was at that very moment standing beside him in the Oval Office. The solution came in minutes.

Sometimes even an experienced operator cannot produce the desired result, however. When President Eisenhower asked the switchboard to reach his assistant, Sherman Adams, who was driving to New Hampshire, the operators calculated where Adams would be, then contacted a farmer at about that place to ask him to flag down a blue Oldsmobile tagged New Hampshire 22. The farmer spotted the car and hailed it, but Adams refused to stop.

President Ford stopped by the White House switchboard in the Old Executive Office Building to thank the operators.

President Kennedy's young daughter Caroline had more luck. When she wanted to speak to Santa Claus, she called the switchboard, and when a repairman working down the hall was pressed into an acting role, she gave him her Christmas list—including a helicopter for her brother who saw their father use one "all the time."

By 1991, the switchboard registered almost 40,000 calls every week. Two or three times that number come in at particularly eventful times such as during the U.S. bombing of Libya in April 1986, or during Operation Desert Storm in early 1991. Sometimes the switchboard is inundated for reasons unrelated to national events. When a television evangelist encouraged viewers to call the President, thousands of them did, swamping the switchboard for hours.

Since the Nixon years, volunteers have assisted the switchboard staff in answering calls directed to the President. Typically political supporters of the incumbent Chief Executive, they answer routine queries, direct callers to a particular source, and keep a tally of opinions expressed. These same unpaid workers address the President's greeting cards, which are sent out each year to wish people happy birthday and happy anniversary. In 1990 the Bushes mailed more than 750,000 of these cards.

If the President and his staff had only telephone messages to answer, their load would be considerably lighter, but many Americans choose to write letters to the President with their opinions, concerns, and requests. As the population of the nation has grown, letters to the White House have multiplied. President Reagan received more than four million written communications in 1986, a far cry from the few that appeared on George Washington's desk when the Republic was young.

Actually the number of letters has grown remarkably even when the population has remained almost static. In 1954–60, President Eisenhower received about 700,000 letters annually; in the 1960s that figure doubled, and by the 1970s the Carter White House reported about 3.5 million each year. By the time George Bush took office, the number had risen to six million.

The letters come in foreign languages (these are forwarded to the State Department for translation), in Braille (answered in Braille), in the awkward block printing of young children (these writers receive a booklet telling them how the White House operates), and in the cramped, careful script of people needing help (these are referred to appropriate agencies).

Perhaps the President's high visibility (and that of his family) make the White House an easy focus for the people's wrath. Certainly its address is easy—probably the only location in the United States for which postal authorities need only two words—White House. The city and street location are superfluous, and even a zip code is deemed unnecessary on White House stationery. In at least one case, just a sketch sufficed. Theodore Roosevelt, whose toothy grin was as famous in his time as Jimmy Carter's became later, received an envelope addressed only with a simple drawing of teeth.

If architect James Hoban could stroll through the White House offices two hundred years after the cornerstone of the mansion was laid, he would see flickering computer terminals on many desks. After the White House Information Systems was set up in the early 1960s to improve communication, the first functions to be computerized were those of national security and military operations. The office staff continued to rely on typewriters and telephones.

The Carter years brought change. Just as personal computers moved into many American homes, they also entered the President's House. Terminals appeared on desks to help schedule cabinet meetings, analyze federal budget data, and create a digital version of the President's signature on letters. The visitors' office and the Curator relied on computers, and by 1982 the clerical staff had learned to use them as well. Finally upper echelon management were assigned terminals on which they could hook up to wire services, peruse personnel and financial data, and contact one another.

Last of all, the President got his own personal computer. In April 1991 George Bush became the first Chief Executive to have a fully automated office—although he gave little indication that he meant to master the new technology. Weeks after the terminal's arrival, his Press Office announced that he had had little time to familiarize himself with it and that his first lesson had involved nothing more than learning how to turn it on. First Lady Barbara Bush was already ahead of her husband in this respect, having become adept at using her compact laptop computer.

★★★

Although he was inaugurated at the Capitol, Richard Nixon gave his resignation speech in the White House and then walked to a helicopter on the South Lawn.

While the President's office is in the White House, the presidential oath of office is rarely taken there. That ceremony is reserved for the Capitol, and only under very special circumstances has a presidential inauguration occurred at 1600 Pennsylvania Avenue. Vice presidents who succeed to the office following the death of the incumbent are sworn in wherever they are, and Harry Truman took his oath in the Cabinet Room of the West Wing after Franklin Roosevelt's death in April 1945. Duly elected Chief Executives rarely had that option.

Rutherford B. Hayes's inauguration, in March 1877, is one of the exceptions. He had won the presidency in a very close election —a special commission had ruled him victorious over the Democrat Samuel Tilden, who actually got more popular votes—and some people expected trouble when Hayes took office. The date of the inauguration that year fell on a Sunday and so two oathtakings were planned. The first—unannounced even to people who were dining in the White House that Saturday night—took place in the Green Room, and then a public ceremony followed at the Capitol on Monday.

White House inaugurations remained rarities until the 1940s

President Harry Truman talked with former
First Lady Eleanor Roosevelt at his desk in
the West Wing Oval Office.

and '50s, when there were two. In both cases incumbents were involved, so there was no question of the nation being without a Chief Executive, even for a very short time. Franklin Roosevelt's fourth term began in January 1945, while World War II continued and the President, seriously ill, prepared to travel to the Soviet Union to meet with Churchill and Stalin at Yalta for peace talks. An extravagant or time-consuming inauguration seemed inappropriate and so a simple, practical ceremony was held at the White House. Crowds watched from a snow-covered South Lawn as Franklin Roosevelt appeared briefly on the portico and took the oath for an unprecedented fourth time.

In 1957 Dwight Eisenhower's second inauguration, which also fell on a Sunday, took place first in the East Room but was reenacted later in a public ceremony on Capitol Hill. The White House ceremony was a very private affair, and Pat Nixon, wife of the Vice President-elect, was called upon to hold the family Bible for her husband's swearing-in. She inadvertently set an example that her successors followed; and after Lady Bird Johnson held the Bible for her husband in 1965, the tradition became established that spouses would participate in the inaugural ceremony.

Neither this nor any other aspect of the First Lady's job had been spelled out in the Constitution. Her role gradually evolved from a purely social one to one with considerable clout, and Americans came to take for granted that the spouse of the Chief Executive would become involved in the administration in very visible and potentially valuable ways. Eleanor Roosevelt called herself "the eyes and ears" who could observe for her husband and report back to him. Lady Bird Johnson, with the assistance of a large and competent staff, made her "Beautification" program an important part of Lyndon Johnson's legislation package.

The stage for the emergence of strong First Ladies had been set in the early days of the Republic when George Washington decided to combine office and residence. Wives of men who work at home would understand why many presidential spouses complained that they could not avoid being drawn into political discussions. Talk concerning problems that the nation faced surrounded them each day. Virtually no visitor paid a purely social call; each came with a business motive.

Every invitation issued from the President's House carried polit-

One of the most activist First Ladies, Eleanor Roosevelt is shown here with the President outside the Oval Office.

ical consequences, and each First Lady who participated in the scheduling of social events entered a partisan thicket. How she manipulated her way through the maze of party alignments and personal enmities could affect her husband's record. Dolley Madison went out of her way to treat opponents as kindly as supporters, and historians credited her as being an important part in James Madison's reelection to the presidency in 1812. Mary Lincoln, less shrewd in such matters, caused her husband some trouble as when, for example, she demanded that guests enter the White House through designated doors, according to their official titles. Judges, senators, and foreign ministers were to be separated from congressional representatives and common folk.

More than social planning was involved if a First Lady wanted to be an asset to her husband. Americans learned to approach the President by making their requests to his wife. As soon as the First Lady became a familiar figure, through coverage in national magazines and newspapers, letters addressed directly to her came in asking for advice and help on everything from temperance to polygamy.

Not until the 1950s did Congress recognize the office of First Lady and supply it with a staff. Presidents' wives before that time were left to fend for themselves: providing their own secretarial help, asking friends to volunteer time, or borrowing workers from other government offices. In the 1870s, when men still monopolized secretarial positions at the White House, Julia Grant employed a man as secretary. Explaining to a reporter why she preferred working with him rather than with a woman, she noted that a woman "might in the beginning prove a perfectly seaworthy vessel but after all, without any warning, spring a leak."

Edith Roosevelt deserves credit for being the first to acquire a secretary at government expense to assist with the First Lady's responsibilities. In 1901 Isabella Hagner, who had previously worked for a relative of Edith Roosevelt, came "on loan" from the clerical section of the War Department. Conditions were so crowded that she had to set up a desk in the First Lady's bedroom and then move "bag and baggage" to the hall when Mrs. Roosevelt needed the room. It was Isabella Hagner who handed out information to reporters on social events—the food and beverages served, the attire of the guests, and the flower arrangements.

Edith Roosevelt's example evidently inspired successive First Ladies to communicate directly with the press rather than to rely entirely on their husbands' staffs. Florence Harding once even invited women reporters up to her second-floor bedroom where she received them in a rose negligée.

Eleanor Roosevelt took women reporters on a tour of the mansion the day after her husband's inauguration and set the following Monday morning at eleven for her first news conference in the Red Room. For the next twelve years she met with reporters regularly whenever she was in Washington. As many as seventy-five women showed up, and the conferences moved from one room in the White House to another—sometimes the Green Room on the main floor or the Monroe Room on the second floor. The First Lady would enter last, often still in riding clothes, and pass around a box of candy or serve some lemonade.

The First Lady's staff remained small until the 1960s but its

As part of her job as First Lady, Jacqueline Kennedy inspected plans for Lafayette Square, on the north side of the White House.

First Lady Rosalynn Carter maintained her own office
in the East Wing.

growth is easily documented. In 1953 the *Congressional Directory* showed official recognition of the distaff side of the White House when it listed as part of the Executive Office one "Acting Secretary to the President's wife." Jacqueline Kennedy hired her own press secretary (another first), and Lady Bird Johnson assembled the largest and most accomplished First Lady's staff in history. The exact number of people working for Mrs. Johnson and her projects remains in doubt. Some came "on loan" from federal agencies and remained for years without ever going on the First Lady's payroll. Others appeared for temporary stints and then left when the job was done.

Located in the East Wing, near the Correspondence Office where invitations are addressed, the office of the First Lady has become an important component of the President's office. Rosalynn Carter, who sometimes went there in a business suit and frequently mentioned the "working lunches" that she shared with the President, helped define the job as a separate and important one. Both Barbara Bush and Nancy Reagan kept an office in the family quarters, and each First Lady maintained a busy schedule involving projects she had chosen to support, speaking engagements, and meetings. By 1990 much of the information about how the White House operated and all photographs of the President's family came not from the West Wing but from the First Lady's Press Office.

★ ★ ★

Large as it has become, the office of the First Lady is only a tiny part of the President's Office, which extends outside the White House compound into surrounding office buildings and across the city, encompassing a complex network of advisers and messages, equipment and responsibilities. Only a fraction of the work accredited to the Chief Executive actually occurs at 1600 Pennsylvania Avenue. After two hundred years, the White House has come to mean not just a place or a job, but a large and powerful operation.

MUSEUM OF A NATION

★ A beautiful classically designed building, the White House makes an impressive showcase for the nation's treasures, its prized collection of period furniture and artwork. Portrait gallery of Presidents and exhibition hall of fine antiques, it contains furnishings of historic as well as artistic interest. Visitors walking through the public rooms immediately sense that they are in a museum—high ceilings and roped-off walkways make this house seem too grand for everyday living and too gracious for an office. The aura of history is strong, and even First Lady Jacqueline Kennedy expressed awe at walking near objects that had belonged to legendary past residents—their influence remained so strong, she said, that for her first two years in the White House she rarely spoke above a whisper.

The Lincoln Bedroom exhibits furniture, artwork, and documents of the period 1850–70.

In November 1988 the American Association of Museums accredited the White House as a museum, thus giving a nod of approval granted to only about one tenth of all institutions in the country that call themselves museums. That decision was not automatic; it followed a two-year review of White House operations and the care of its collections. The Association concluded that the President's House had moved beyond being simply a home and office for the Chief Executive and had become, in the words of one scholar, "the nation's oldest important showcase for the arts." From now on it would have to answer to more than its occupants whenever a change of furnishings or decoration was considered.

No complete catalogue of White House holdings exists, but if one could be designed from the computerized inventory it would be immense, including thousands of items in several categories: furniture (1,942), ceramics (15,661); glassware (3,145); metalware (13,092); lighting fixtures (1,121); paintings (338); prints and drawings (451); and sculpture (69). The list requires regular updating as new donations and acquisitions arrive.

For nearly a century, occupants of the President's House gave little attention to preserving its historical record. In 1801 John Adams carefully listed the furnishings right before his presidential term was up, but he was probably motivated more by the need to protect himself against charges of theft than by the wisdom of starting an archive. His successors were no more systematic than he, and few of them left anything beyond sketchy descriptions of the various rooms. Historians trying to reconstruct the mansion's appearance at a particular time must turn to letters, government vouchers, and cryptically written notes that survive from that period.

As it neared its one-hundredth birthday in 1892—and perhaps because of this milestone—the White House began to take on historic importance of its own, and occupants, especially First Ladies, tried to compile a record of the building's past. Lucretia Garfield set out to research the topic in the Library of Congress in 1881 because, her husband wrote in his diary, "so little is known." But she soon became ill with malaria, and before she had recovered, her husband was assassinated, thus ending any scholarship on the mansion she may have envisioned.

The first archival projects of Presidents' wives centered on prized collectors' pieces used by previous administrations, and books about the White House focused on the people who lived and worked there. Nineteenth-century historians and Executive Mansion employees penned dozens of volumes, detailing their research, experiences, and opinions, but no one catalogued the physical objects. Even in 1908, when Gilson Willets published *Inside History of the White House*, he devoted more pages to "Relatives as First Ladies" and "Holidays at the White House" than to "Public and Private Rooms" or "White House Portraits."

Not until the 1920s was any concerted effort made to document the mansion's holdings and to attract donations that would enhance its archival significance. Grace Coolidge, stymied by her husband in so many of her personal projects during her years as First Lady, set an important precedent when she appointed the first advisory committee ever named to oversee the selection of furnishings and artwork for the White House. The First Lady wisely chose experts with broad experience as collectors, donors, and advisers

Lady Bird Johnson, in a small ceremony in the East Room in June 1964, accepted a donation to the White House Collection.

at other historic sites and at the newly opened American Wing of New York's Metropolitan Museum of Art.

Grace Coolidge's project focused on the family quarters, but since furniture and artworks were moved from one floor to another at residents' requests, she had to consider furnishings for the entire mansion. Money was a major consideration, and in 1925 an obliging legislature increased appropriations from the twenty thousand dollars routinely granted each new administration to fifty thousand dollars, the same amount that is allocated today to each incoming family for redecorating their own quarters. Even in the 1920s that sum was insufficient to purchase valuable furnishings to upgrade the interior, and so Congress passed additional legislation permitting the First Lady and her committee to seek donations directly from private sources, as a typical museum staff does.

Because of a combination of personalities and events, Grace Coolidge never attained the reputation of Jacqueline Kennedy as restorer of the White House. Mrs. Coolidge's Advisory Committee members disagreed over what kind of furniture was preferable, and a national debate erupted over whether "colonial" styles were more appropriate to the mansion than "Victorian" pieces or those identified with beaux arts or "foreign" designs. Americans who had never before given much thought to the subject joined in the argument, and one magazine invited its readers to send in their opinions. Finally President Coolidge abruptly halted the project by announcing that nothing at all would be done. Other than a dozen or so pieces of furniture that were donated and a coverlet that Mrs. Coolidge crocheted for the Lincoln bed, there is little trace left of her project to refurbish the White House.

Learning from the Coolidge experience, successive administrations were slow to embark on new restoration projects. The years of the Great Depression hardly offered the right setting for talk of upgrading the White House, although Lou Hoover did instruct one of her assistants to begin a history of the mansion (never published), and she arranged to have reproductions made of some of President James Monroe's furniture. Mrs. Hoover had admired the pieces that Monroe's descendants had donated to a museum dedicated to their famous ancestor in Fredericksburg, Virginia, and, realizing that the original furniture was unattainable, she had several pieces copied for a parlor that she had set aside for her family on

Delegates from the National Society of Interior Designers presented President and Mrs. Eisenhower with furniture for the Diplomatic Reception Room on the ground floor, the first room to be furnished entirely with authentic antiques.

the second floor. Coincidentally, the Monroes had designated that room for the same use, and the Hoovers initiated the practice of calling it the Monroe Room.

The two subsequent Presidents did not continue the Hoover restoration project. Franklin Roosevelt proposed including a separate museum in the new East Wing (built in 1942 and eventually the location of the office of the First Lady), and Harry Truman endorsed the idea, but neither Eleanor Roosevelt nor Bess Truman indicated much interest.

By the late 1950s, attitudes appeared to be changing. Just as Dwight and Mamie Eisenhower prepared to retire to their Gettysburg farm, the National Society of Interior Designers [NSID] donated furniture for the Diplomatic Reception Room (so named because diplomats traditionally gathered there in the oval room on the ground floor). The NSID had worked two years to collect the necessary funds (about $100,000) and to locate enough appropriate pieces to furnish this room entirely in "early American antiques." It was the only room in the White House, the designers noted proudly, with that distinction.

With the publicity surrounding the arrival of the furniture in June 1960, an idea may have been planted in the mind of Jacqueline Kennedy, whose husband was about to capture the Democratic party's nomination for President. Almost immediately after John Kennedy's election in November, his wife announced her project as First Lady—to make the White House a "showcase of American art and history." Only three years (to the day) intervened between that announcement and President Kennedy's assassination, but it was

Jacqueline Kennedy conducted camera crews on a preview tour of the White House prior to filming a televised tour in early 1962.

time enough for her to build a reputation as the most successful of the several First Ladies who attempted to restore the White House.

Jacqueline Kennedy set the stage for an entirely new way of viewing the White House. In January 1961 she named a twelve-member committee to help locate appropriate furniture and works of art and to raise the money for further purchases. A few months later Lorraine Pearce, a twenty-six-year-old curator on loan from the Smithsonian Institution, went to work full-time cataloguing everything in the building. Congress put its own important stamp of approval on the project by passing a law to make removal of objects difficult: "furniture, fixtures and decorative objects of the White House, when declared by the President to be of historic or artistic interest," would be permanent—future occupants could not discard them at whim.

Public enthusiasm was enormous, and hundreds of donations came in. Some were large, others very small. One fourth grader in Kansas sent a dollar and encouraged his friends to contribute too, so that more antiques and paintings could be purchased.

President Kennedy, sensitive to the political consequences associated with projects termed "elitist," hesitated to endorse the restoration program, and Mrs. Kennedy wrote that she was "warned, begged, and practically threatened" not to undertake it. She persisted, she explained publicly, because she wanted the house to be one that all Americans could take pride in, and she wanted schoolchildren especially to understand its significance. Jacqueline Kennedy had first visited the White House when she was eleven years old, and she remembered being impressed by its uniqueness. Returning in 1960 for a private tour with Mamie Eisenhower, Mrs. Kennedy had an entirely different reaction; she confided to a friend that she had been disappointed with the undistinguished furnishings, some of them in rather worn condition.

In order for the restoration project to support itself, a guidebook to the White House was published and put on sale in the summer of 1962. Since the sales actually occurred on White House premises, complaints about "commercialization" came in, but success at the cash register mitigated the sting of disapproval. At one dollar per copy, the guidebooks sold well and nearly two million of them were printed in the next two years.

The organization that actually oversaw the project was the

White House Historical Association, formed in November 1961 under the First Lady's aegis for the purpose of increasing "the understanding, appreciation, and enjoyment of the Executive Mansion." The Association also collected private funds to be used for purchasing items that would enhance the collection—whether a painting, a piece of furniture, or an important document.

In 1961 the White House began a systematic listing of every new acquisition, and three years later it published a catalogue or inventory, setting a precedent that later administrations would follow. Each item in the catalogue had a number, indicating the date it was "accessioned," and a description, including size, period, materials, and the source that provided it for the President's House. For example, a mahogany writing table, made in America "circa 1850" and measuring thirty-six inches wide and twenty-six inches deep was described as "Victorian, with rectangular top covered in black leather. Single drawer opening in front with Victorian gilt pulls. Four cabriole legs carved at knees and feet." Julia Grant had used the desk as First Lady, and it was donated in 1961 by a couple who lived in South Wellfleet, Massachusetts.

The catalogue divided its new holdings into four categories (Furniture, Furnishings, Fine Arts, Documents) and then subdivided each of these into twenty-two smaller groups. Among the forty-seven chairs donated to the White House in 1961 was one armchair from the original set that President Monroe had ordered from France in 1817. Six chairs were purchased with "general funds" and although none of them could be directly connected to a White House family, all were excellent examples of American craftsmanship around 1800.

Jacqueline Kennedy went in "working clothes" to look through White House storage rooms and sort out those pieces worthy of display. Some valuable items, formerly kept under lock and key except for the most important visitors, went on permanent exhibit for every tourist to see. The enormous gilt plateau centerpiece, comprising seven sections capable of extension to thirteen feet, which had impressed dinner guests at the President's House since 1817 and had been described as "the chief historic treasure of the White House," was now set out on the table for all visitors to admire.

Jacqueline Kennedy's personal popularity drew people to the

White House where they viewed the dazzling vermeil collection which the Eisenhowers had quietly put on display in 1957. Margaret Thompson Biddle, an American heiress who spent years in Paris accumulating artwork and silver had died the previous year, and although some of her estate was auctioned off in Europe, much of the vermeil collection had been willed to the American President's House. Vermeil, a process in which silver pieces are dipped in gold, had been popular in 1817 when President Monroe bought furnishings for the Executive Mansion, and he included vermeil flatware in his order. The Biddle gift, valued at $100,000, would complement what remained of Monroe's original order, and its urns and trays would become the focus of one entire room's exhibit on the ground floor.

The Vermeil Room on the ground floor highlights the White House collection of vermeil (gold-dipped silver).

During the Kennedy administration the White House was transformed into a fledgling museum with its own curator, advisory committee of experts, and fund-raising outfit, but it took the endorsement of successive administrations to ensure the development of the collection. Lyndon Johnson cooperated by signing an important executive order: one part created a Committee for the Preservation of the White House to advise on the "museum character" of the public rooms so that the House could become "a living testament to the history of our country"; the second section provided for a full-time curator to be appointed by the President.

Now that the White House holdings were protected by the 1961 law, Americans more willingly donated treasured objects. CBS turned over the microphone used by Franklin Roosevelt for his Fireside Chats. A Salt Lake City attorney sent in a dinner plate that he said had been a gift to his uncle from Theodore Roosevelt more than fifty years earlier. The plate's purple border surrounding an American eagle established it as part of the dinner service purchased for the White House by Mary Lincoln. According to the donor's letter, his uncle, a Boston newspaper editor, had been accompanying President Roosevelt through the White House one day and had noticed the plates. When he announced that his wife would be "thrilled" to own one, T.R. obligingly opened the cupboard and handed one over.

While donations of historic White House items were welcomed, such pieces were not sufficient to raise the collection to the showcase status that its backers envisioned. The Committee for the Preservation of the White House actively sought additions, making specific requests for portraits of Presidents and their wives, as well as paintings by such distinguished American artists as Mary Cassatt, Thomas Eakins, and George Caleb Bingham.

In January 1967, Joseph Hirshhorn, a New York philanthropist who owned a large collection of Eakins paintings, obligingly donated a 1903 portrait of a young girl. The subject of the painting, which was of enormous value at the time, was Ruth Harding, the niece of one of Eakins's closest friends. Lady Bird Johnson was delighted with the gift and saw that it immediately went on display in one of the public rooms, but she was somewhat nonplussed a short time later when, escorting a group of visitors, she remarked how sad the painting's young subject looked. One elderly man in the group spoke up in Ruth Harding's defense—she really was not a sad woman at all, he said, and he should know because he married her.

During the Nixon administration, efforts to restore the White House continued—in fact, they accelerated. A new curator, Clement E. Conger, was appointed in early 1970, and he brought a remarkable enthusiasm and singleness of purpose to the job. Complaining of Congress's stinginess with "the most important house in the world," he described himself as "passionately dedicated" to transforming the mansion into the world's finest repository of American art and antiques.

Besides the lack of money, Conger encountered other problems as White House Curator. He found that each new First Family had quite different ideas about what furnishings they wanted on the second floor of the residence. Jacqueline Kennedy put wallpaper featuring scenes from the American Revolution in the family dining room, but Betty Ford had the paper removed and painted the room yellow. The scenes were inaccurate anyway, a history buff pointed out—the nineteenth-century French artist had placed battles at sites where none had occurred.

Almost immediately on assuming the curatorship, Conger created a stir by telling the *New York Times* that Jacqueline Kennedy's contribution to White House restoration had been exaggerated by the press who had "created an optical illusion that the White House contained a great collection of American antiques." Conger was particularly critical of Stephane Boudin, the Frenchman who had advised Mrs. Kennedy on wall coverings and draperies for the public rooms on the state floor. Boudin's previous experience had been at Malmaison, and Conger judged him untrained in restoring American period houses. The result was more French than American, critics charged, and Conger initiated what became known to insiders as the "de-Kennedyization" of the White House. He began with the Green and Red rooms, and during the next five years all the principal rooms on the main and ground floors were redecorated to reflect the views of Conger and the Committee for the Preservation of the White House.

The Green Room may have gained its designated color before any of the other rooms, since Thomas Jefferson (who dined there)

First Lady Pat Nixon conferred with Curator Clement Conger on paintings added to the White House Collection.

133

The Green Room, furnished in the Federal style,
boasts many fine pieces that date from 1800–15.

and the Monroes (who made it their Card Room) all used green floor coverings, upholstery, and draperies. Under Clement Conger's direction, the room was refurbished in 1971 and furnished with outstanding pieces from the first two decades of the White House's use. Duncan Phyfe, the nineteenth-century Scottish cabinetmaker who made a reputation for himself in New York, is represented by several pieces, including the desk-bookcase on the south wall; and Lawrence Ackerman, who upholstered for Duncan Phyfe, signed one of the chairs. The two mahogany worktables near the fireplace conceal multiple tiny drawers and compartments which, when opened out, form a labyrinth of intricate workmanship. The early Presidents are well represented: the Sheffield silver coffee urn on the long table in front of the sofa once belonged to John and Abigail Adams; and the marble mantel, moved here from the State Dining Room, is one of James Monroe's purchases.

Another of the marble mantels ordered by Monroe is in the Red Room, a favorite parlor of Dolley Madison (interestingly, the room was decorated in yellow when she was First Lady). Furnished in the American Empire style of 1810–30, the Red Room is the setting for one of the most important and best documented pieces of furniture the White House owns from those years: a small round table, labeled by its maker Charles-Honoré Lannuier, is made of mahogany and other woods, its marble top of magnificent geometric inlay and its legs exquisitely curved. This room frequently served for musical performances in the nineteenth century, and coincidentally the Empire style featured the stringed lyre as a decorative motif in chair backs and table legs.

Refurbishing these state rooms required public and private support, and Clement Conger, in appealing to Americans to donate rare antiques, gave multiple reasons for doing so: tax deductions, national pride, and family pride. Sometimes it takes all three, he admitted. His plea for donations became all the more important when he found himself shut out of competitive bidding for fine furniture and artwork that came up for sale. He simply could not match the prices offered by well-heeled collectors buying for themselves.

During Jimmy Carter's presidency important American paintings were added to the White House collection, and when he left as

President in 1981 the time seemed right for major refurbishing of the second floor. To help cover expenses, a fund drive was organized, and after the original goal of $850,000 was quickly reached, a total of $1.2 million in private contributions came in. This money, augmented by sums raised by the White House Historical Association and funds appropriated by Congress, provided for painting the exterior, conservation treatment of 150 objects inside, and purchase of additional artworks.

The refurbishing of the private quarters alone cost $730,000 and provided new wall coverings in ten rooms, seven closets, and eight bathrooms. The master bedroom was decorated with hand-painted wallpaper in eighteenth century style. Thirty-three mahogany doors were refinished, as were the floors in twenty-four rooms. Eighteen carpets were replaced, along with many draperies and lamp shades.

Congress agreed to pay for restoring the White House exterior and work began in 1980 with plans for completion by 1992. This complicated stone cleaning, which started on the east wall and concluded on the west façade, required that the mansion wear unattractive scaffolding for more than a decade. Visitors making their first trip to Washington would have to choose their photo backgrounds carefully, since much of the mansion was covered up. In fact, tourists' comments might have echoed those of a woman who, during the 1920s renovation, mistook the scaffolding for a fire escape and concluded that the White House must be a real firetrap.

Cleaning revealed many details in the stone façade and enhanced the building's appearance. Multiple coats of paint (as many as thirty-two in some places) had been put on top of the first layer that had been used to seal the porous Virginia sandstone in 1798. Intricate carvings at the tops of the windows and on the pilasters and columns had been completely obscured, and twisted ropes and delicate roses, the result of months of skillful chiseling, had disappeared under multiple coats of white paint.

After experts settled on a complicated process combining a chemical stripper with a water spray, hunks of paint came off, revealing delicate molding and "tooth tooling" that formed tiny ridges. Remnants of paint remained, but workmen proceeded cautiously, using special plastic scrapers so as to avoid causing further damage. After the stonework had been repaired, the entire surface was ready to be painted with two coats of a specially tailored formula, but restorers decided to leave uncovered one small section under a north window, where ominous scorch marks from the burning by the British in the War of 1812 were still visible.

These markings remind Americans that the White House is a unique record of their past, and whenever anyone suggests altering its basic structure, objections are heard loud and clear. More than once (and with most publicity in the 1890s, 1920s, and 1940s), elaborate plans were drawn up to change the exterior significantly, adding new wings to accommodate an expanded office on the west side and an extensive museum on the east side. Each time the plan was scrapped so that the basic dimensions of the White House remained as they were drawn in the 1790s.

The Library on the ground floor houses a large selection of books by American writers on American topics.

The Blue Room contains several pieces of furniture
ordered for it by President James Monroe in 1817.

Opinions were mixed on the results. One visitor noted that the straw carpet on the second-floor Oval Room was filthy from tobacco juice that had missed the spittoons, but another described the East Room as "fit for a king." Economy, more than aesthetics, shaped judgments about what hung on the walls and filled the rooms, and Presidents had no qualms about discarding things they did not like or sending wagonloads off for auction.

By 1860 Empire furnishings had gone out of style, and President Buchanan sold most of the Monroe furniture. Not until the 1960s—when the White House made an effort to bring back furniture originally purchased by the Presidents rather than accept reproductions or period pieces—did much of the Monroe furniture reappear. One settee and seven chairs in the Blue Room are the same ones that Monroe bought—and plaques on the backs of four chairs identify them as the work of French cabinetmaker Pierre-Antoine Bellangé.

Buchanan and other late-nineteenth-century Presidents preferred the massive, ornately carved pieces that marked the most stylish interiors of their time. Woodworking machines had been perfected to turn out elaborate carvings of curlicues and flowers, and the most fashionable furniture revealed—even flaunted—this new technology. President Buchanan and his niece Harriet Lane ordered several pieces in this Victorian rococo-revival style and they transformed the Blue Room with plush, heavily upholstered chairs and sofas. Not everyone approved of Buchanan's choices even then, and a New York reporter described the fringes, flowers, and tufts as "a perfect *cholera morbus* of drapery and furniture."

The Lincoln suite on the second floor of the White House exhibits outstanding examples of the Victorian style and serves as a memorial to the martyred President. The centerpiece is a dark rosewood bed with an ornate headboard so high that it seems more fitting for a throne. Although the Lincolns bought the bed, they probably never used it, in spite of the fact that its size—eight feet long and six feet wide—suggests that it may have been purchased with the tall President in mind. Other furniture in these two rooms, which once served him as offices, touched Lincoln's life in some way: a chair resembling the one he sat in at Ford's Theatre the night he was shot; chairs used by his cabinet members at meetings; the desk he wrote at while staying at the summer White House a few

This portrait of Angelica Van Buren, painted in 1842 after she left the White House, hangs in the Red Room, furnished in the Empire style, 1810–30.

miles away. The desk displays Lincoln's most famous words—the Gettysburg Address, the only copy in existence that he titled, signed, and dated.

Mary Lincoln bought extravagantly for the White House (exceeding by $6,700 the normal $20,000 allotment made by Congress), and her husband protested. It "would stink in the nostrils of the American people," he explained, if he approved an overrun for the purchase of plush hassocks or "flub dubs" while Union soldiers went without blankets. The First Lady may have slowed her spending, but finding many merchants willing to extend credit, she continued to buy draperies and linens for the White House and clothing and jewelry for herself.

Subsequent administrations (Johnson, Grant, and Hayes) alternated between frugality and extravagance. One spent heavily on the mansion and the next ignored it, or at least permitted deterioration. The family of Andrew Johnson behaved as though they had been taking the money from their own pockets, whereas the Grants introduced a free hand entirely in keeping with their "Gilded Age," and later Rutherford and Lucy Hayes boasted of rummaging in attics and basement storerooms to furnish the various rooms.

Calling the White House poorly outfitted, Chester Arthur refused to stay there until improvements were made. He auctioned off wagonloads of furniture and engaged his fellow New Yorker Louis Comfort Tiffany to design a huge screen of colored glass for the front hall.

Tiffany's ornate style survived until the state floor was completely redecorated during Theodore Roosevelt's presidency. In place of the dark, heavy furnishings and wall coverings, the Roosevelts chose simple shapes and light colors. The East Room was left largely unfurnished; its gleaming parquet floors and elegant Steinway grand piano seemed adequate adornment. Ellen Slayden, wife of a Southern congressman, remarked that the White House had been transformed from "a gilded barn" into a comfortable residence.

★★★

From the very beginning, portraits had been considered vital to the White House collection, and they account for much of the feeling of being in a museum that visitors have as they walk through the mansion. The famous full-length portrait of George Washington that hangs in the East Room is only one of many that Gilbert Stuart produced of the nation's first President. Another, more familiar portrait—since it approximates the one on the dollar bill—hangs in a different room. The East Room painting is actually a copy that Stuart produced of an earlier portrait done while Washington was alive, and it has some unusual features. The mouth is clenched, and at least one friend of Washington stated that it was not a good likeness.

The portrait of George Washington in the East Room is best known as the sole artwork that survives from the Executive Mansion prior to August 24, 1814, the date when Dolley Madison provided

Visitors gathered in the East Room for music, dances, and receptions.

Louis Comfort Tiffany designed this large screen for the White House main entrance hall in 1882.

for its rescue. President James Madison had been out inspecting his troops that day—every indication pointed to a British assault on the capital—but the First Lady refused to leave the White House and even flouted the prospect of danger by ordering that the dinner table be set for forty guests. Friends solicitous of her safety urged her to flee, and Dolley admitted in a letter to her sister that one of them is "in a very bad humor with me because I insist on waiting until the large picture of Gen. Washington is secured." Finally, after making one last tour of the state rooms where she salvaged small silver items that she could take with her, Dolley Madison left, confident that the portrait was safe.

Always one of the most prized possessions of the White House, the painting of George Washington inspired later Presidents to have their likenesses done. James Monroe, who as Secretary of State had responsibility for such matters, commissioned John Vanderlyn, who had studied with Gilbert Stuart, to do President Madison's portrait. For his own portrait as Chief Executive, Monroe turned to Samuel F. B. Morse, the man better known to later generations as the inventor of the telegraph.

Additions were made sporadically to the White House portrait gallery until 1857 when Congress commissioned George P. A. Healy, one of the country's foremost portraitists, to do several of the unrepresented Presidents. Healy completed portraits of John Quincy Adams, Martin Van Buren, James Polk, Millard Fillmore, Franklin Pierce, and John Tyler, but after the War between the States started, money was not available to have the pictures framed. After the war ended, Andrew Johnson's daughter, who found the canvases rolled up in the attic, arranged for their framing and display in the large transverse hall on the state floor. This came about, ironically, because the President, who was a poorly educated man and the only Chief Executive to be impeached (but not convicted), took great pleasure in showing visitors through the Presidents' portrait gallery.

Very quickly the collection of paintings outgrew the main hall. Only a few of the nation's Chief Executives, often the most recent, enjoy the honor of being represented in the heavily traveled first-floor corridor. Other portraits, the works of a distinguished roster of American painters, appear throughout various rooms of the residence, and favorites of the incumbent hang in the Cabinet Room of

George Washington's portrait by Gilbert Stuart has been hanging in the White House since 1800 — the only item to have been there so long. (detail)

the West Wing. Healy's famous portrait of Abraham Lincoln commands a special place above the mantel in the State Dining Room, and another picture, a miniature of President Lincoln and his son Tad, hangs in the Lincoln Bedroom. The latter was probably done in the 1870s and is the work of Francis Carpenter, who had stayed at the Lincoln White House for several months to paint a picture of the President and his cabinet as they appeared at the time of the signing of the Emancipation Proclamation. On meeting Carpenter for the first time Lincoln had asked skeptically, "Do you think you can make a handsome picture of me?"

Posing for an official portrait becomes part of every President's job, although most delay it until leaving office. Jimmy Carter sat for painter Herbert E. Abrams in 1982, more than a year after leaving Washington, D.C., and although he appears seated in a chair from the Red Room, Carter actually posed in Plains, Georgia. Gerald Ford's portrait was painted in 1977 by Everett Kinstler while the ex-President was at his home in Vail, Colorado.

More than one Chief Executive has had second thoughts about his official portrait after it was finished. Lyndon Johnson made headlines by rejecting the one done of him by Peter Hurd. Commissioned by the White House Historical Association (at a reported fee of six thousand dollars, which was half of Hurd's usual price for a color portrait), the painting took several months to complete. When Hurd delivered it to the Johnson ranch in Texas he received a very cool reception. The President greeted him with "icy politeness," Hurd reported, and Lady Bird Johnson described the meeting between the two men as the grimmest she ever expected to witness if she "lived to be one thousand." Johnson called the painting "the ugliest thing I ever saw" and showed the artist a likeness he much preferred—one done by the popular illustrator Norman Rockwell. The President's opinion no doubt explains its banishment from the White House, although the First Lady's office gave other reasons: it was "inappropriate" (with the Capitol in the background), not consistent in style with other Presidents' portraits, and (at 40 inches by 48 inches) "too big."

Lyndon Johnson was not the only person to worry about how he would appear in the permanent White House gallery. Richard Nixon switched portraits after leaving office, preferring one by J.

The main stairway near the North Entrance serves also as portrait galley for ex-Presidents.

Edith Roosevelt posed for only a portion of this portrait painted by Théobald Chartran while she was First Lady.

Anthony Wills, who had also done Eisenhower's portrait. In 1991 Ronald Reagan sent a portrait of himself done by Everett Kinstler to replace one done earlier by Aaron Shikler. Calvin Coolidge took more time to change his mind. At the conclusion of his presidency he left a portrait in which he appeared dressed in a cutaway coat; three years later he returned to retrieve it and replace it with one that showed him in a business suit.

Coolidge, known for his thrift, did not cut corners when it came to portraits. He had expected to sit for the painter Howard Chandler Christy, but finding a full schedule that day, he arranged for his wife to be the subject. That portrait, showing the vivacious First Lady in a red dress standing beside her collie Rob Roy, is very much a product of the 1920s; the dog's name—also the name of a cocktail—is a spoof on the prohibition decade.

Since 1902 the entry corridor on the ground floor has exhibited portraits of the First Ladies.

148

At least the First Lady posed for it herself. In 1902, Edith Roosevelt arranged to have her portrait painted by Théobald Chartran, but finding that her large family and busy White House schedule left her too little time, she prevailed on a friend of roughly the same body proportions to substitute for her. The First Lady posed only while her face was being sketched, and that may account for the fact that neither she nor her husband liked the finished product. Such substitutions were fairly common. In 1878 when President Hayes asked his Ohio artist friend Eliphalet F. Andrews to do a portrait of Martha Washington to hang as a companion to the full-length portrait of George Washington, a niece of Hayes, Emily Platt, served as the model.

By the time the Executive Mansion had been officially renamed the White House in 1902, Presidents' wives had become prominent national figures, and Edith Roosevelt thought it appropriate to organize a portrait gallery featuring them all ("myself included," she specified) on the ground floor. The wide corridor seemed a perfect place for exhibiting portraits, and although not all White House wives left their likenesses—some of those from the nineteenth century provided no painting or photograph or drawing even for their own children—all since 1869 (except Ellen Wilson) are represented in the White House collection.

Jacqueline Kennedy's portrait, one of those eagerly sought by tourists, often meets puzzled responses. The First Lady most closely associated with White House restoration posed for painter Aaron Shikler in her New York apartment, and there is nothing in the painting to connect her with the Executive Mansion or with the energy and vigor that characterized the Kennedy administration. A much-imitated fashion plate when she lived in the White House, Jacqueline Kennedy is shown not in the pillbox hat or simple sleeveless dress that she helped popularize in the early 1960s, but in a full-length, long-sleeved robe that defies identification with any particular period. Actually, she had remarried—becoming the wife of Aristotle Onassis, the Greek shipping tycoon—before this portrait was done in 1970.

Before 1960, White House art was limited almost entirely to portraits of the Presidents and their wives, but during the next three decades the collection widened so that it showed many different regions of the nation. Paintings that now hang in the White House

First Lady Jacqueline Kennedy posed for her official White House portrait in 1970. (detail)

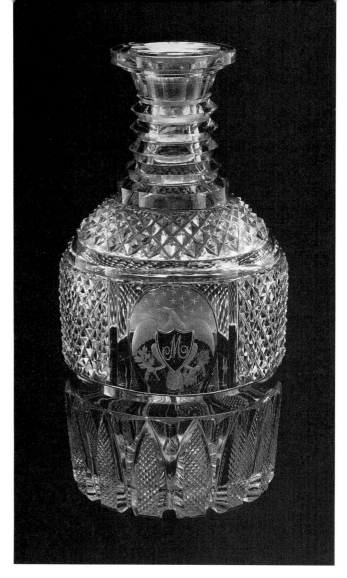

A decanter given to President James Madison in 1816.

include cityscapes of Philadelphia and New York; a Connecticut "Farmyard in Winter"; "Florida Sunrise" (the first Southern scene to be acquired for the White House); "Niagara Falls," and "Cliffs of Green River, Wyoming."

Western themes were favored by President Reagan, and several artworks selected for exhibit in the West Wing during his two terms reflected that interest. The Oval Office boasted a Remington sculpture, "Bronco Buster," and in the lobby were several paintings with Western motifs, including "Crossing the River Platte" and "Point Lobos, Monterey, California." Additional valuable paintings featuring Western subjects came into the White House collection as gifts during the Reagan years—Albert Bierstadt's landscape "View of the Rocky Mountains," and Charles Russell's "Fording the Horse Herd."

Although the White House had a policy of acquiring works of artists no longer living, in 1970 the Nixons drew attention to the White House's collection by holding an exhibit of a contemporary painter. The first one-man show in the building's history featured Andrew Wyeth, a favorite of the President and First Lady. Some of the twenty-one Wyeth paintings that hung in the East Room had never been previously exhibited.

Not all of the painters featured in the White House are American. One of the most poignant reminders of John Kennedy's brief presidency is a painting by a French impressionist that was donated by Kennedy's family in his memory. The work of Claude Monet, "Morning on the Seine," with its misty early morning blue, catches a scene as transitory as the presidency of the man whose memory it honors.

Also of great historic and artistic interest are the china, glassware, and metalware acquired by the White House over two centuries. Remnants of large purchases made by many different Presidents are exhibited in various parts of the public floors—in display cases in the east foyer and on the large table in the State Dining Room.

Among the most fragile White House holdings are the 3,145 pieces of glassware, including 870 surviving from the nineteenth century. This represents only a fraction of what was bought, since many dozens of glasses were broken at receptions and din-

This painting by Claude Monet was a gift to the White House from John F. Kennedy's family, donated in memory of the late President.

ners. Other pieces were given out as mementos of special occasions.

In the earliest days of the nation's capital, European diplomats sold off their household furnishings and silver when departing from their posts, and the President's House could pick up quality silver at bargain prices. No one seemed to mind that it was secondhand. Soon, however, the idea developed that the Executive Mansion deserved its own custom-made or at least specially selected furnishings. In 1826 a federal law mandated that purchases be American-made, unless nothing suitable was available.

A glass compote purchased for the Jackson administration.

Glass-making was among the first skills sufficiently developed in the United States to satisfy White House buyers. In 1817 an Englishman wrote that he was "astonished" to "witness such perfection on this side of the Atlantic" and especially in western Pennsylvania, "that part of America which a New Yorker supposes to be at the farther end of the world."

President Monroe evidently agreed with that assessment because that same year he placed an order for glassware with Benjamin Bakewell, whose factory he had visited the year before. Pittsburgh and the surrounding area had several glass factories, and local residents took pride in their reputation for producing quality products. The *Pittsburgh Gazette* boasted that an order from the President for a full set of "decanters, wine glasses and tumblers of various sizes and different models, exhibiting a brilliant specimen of double flint, engraved and cut by Jardelle," would put the region on the map; the firm of Bakewell & Page was to be congratulated for making Pittsburgh manufactures "known to the world." Not a single glass from that shipment survives—only the bill showing a hefty price of fifteen dollars per dozen for one hundred forty-four "cut Tumblers" with the "U.S. arms engraved on each."

The oldest surviving glassware at the White House was ordered by President Andrew Jackson from the same Pittsburgh firm in 1829. Later Presidents added to the supply with purchases of their own in the flat panel cut glass patterns with engraved vines, grapes, and the American eagle.

Monroe's order and those that followed show how closely the Seal of the United States became associated with the presidency. Most Americans see it often, since it appears on every dollar bill, but few realize that it predates the Constitution. In 1782, when the Revolution was not yet formally concluded, the seal began to appear, showing an eagle (symbolizing authority) holding in one talon a sheaf of arrows (signifying preparedness) and in the other talon an olive branch (symbolizing peace). Thus Americans seemed to be announcing, very early in their struggle toward nationhood, that they were prepared for both war and peace.

Over time the seal would vary in small details, depending on who designed it. The Jackson glassware shows a curious deviation. Although Jackson was known for his belligerent military initiatives, the glassware purchased for his administration featured an eagle devoid of arrows, clutching in one talon a palm frond and in the other a laurel branch.

New Yorker Martin Van Buren had little use for the "plain" table settings of his predecessor in the Executive Mansion, and as soon as he took office in 1837 he began planning elegant dinner parties. The President enjoyed fine wine and evidently had his own ideas about what kind of glasses he wanted to offer his guests. Instead of relying on the Pittsburgh firm for all the necessary glass replacements, Van Buren ordered from importers, thus stirring up many objections. One critical congressman from Pennsylvania, Charles Ogle, complained that the President was "spending the People's cash on *foreign Fanny Kemble green finger cups* in which to wash his pretty tapering, soft, white lily fingers, after dining on *fricandeau de veau* and *omelette soufflé*."

Van Buren did buy some of his countrymen's products, including the first pressed glassware for the mansion. This technique, in which glass is pressed for its shape and design rather than blown, was still a novelty in the 1830s, and American craftsmen were particularly skilled at it. Colored finger bowls were much in vogue in the 1830s, at least among the fashionable, and Van Buren braved Congressman Ogle's disapproval to provide his guests with tiny bowls filled with water and a slice of lemon or an orange leaf.

Other Presidents would add to the glass service, disposing in various ways of the odd pieces left over from their predecessors. Mary Lincoln included in her many purchases an entirely new set of glassware which she specified should be "rich-cut & engraved with the U.S. Coat of Arms." In this case the eagle on the seal reverted to the original pose, wielding both arrows and an olive branch. This pattern endured, with subsequent administrations adding to it over the next four decades, and it held the record as the longest in use.

Many items disappeared in one way or another. Some were broken at crowded receptions or during the process of being washed and stored. Others were probably removed by souvenir hunters who could not resist the chance to walk off with evidence of their visit to the White House. Sometimes odd pieces were sold to help raise money for a new set, and at least one glass in the White House collection is a gift from the descendants of people who happened to find it at an 1850 auction.

By the 1890s styles in glassware had shifted, and thicker, heavier glass forms (called "blanks") were being cut into intricate patterns featuring diamond shapes and stars. One of these "rich-cut" designs, the popular "Russian" pattern, was selected by First Lady Caroline Harrison when she purchased additional glassware in 1891. Although she tried to economize and ordered only sixty of each item, the number of different pieces required by each diner (water goblet, champagne glass, claret, sauterne, sherry, Apollinaris tumbler, finger bowl, and ice cream plate), shows how very complicated a table setting had become. Dinner guests who became bored with the table conversation might have noticed that the eagle in the Harrison glass pattern faced left toward the arrows rather than right, as had been the case with the Lincoln glassware.

In the major refurbishing of the White House in 1902, First Lady Edith Roosevelt changed the way breakables were discarded. She considered it inappropriate that the President's china and

Jacqueline Kennedy's choice of glassware for the White House (left) contrasts sharply with the ornate styles preferred by her predecessors. Mary Lincoln's selection (right), reordered by other Presidents until 1891, featured the presidential seal.

China purchased during the Monroe administration.

glassware could be parceled out to friends or auctioned off to the highest bidder, and so she arranged for a more dignified demise. Any rejects from the pantry, no longer usable because of chips or insufficient numbers, were to be broken in pieces and thrown into the Potomac. One White House aide, an ardent admirer of the First Lady, concurred in her decision although it troubled him to implement it. In a letter to his family, he wrote wistfully: "When I think how I should value even one piece of it, it hurts to smash it, but I am sure it is the only right thing to do."

Subsequent Presidents bought supplements or new glassware in the intricate patterns offered by American firms, until 1961 when Jacqueline Kennedy ordered plain unmarked glassware from Morgantown, West Virginia, not far from where President Monroe had placed an order in 1817. She explained that she wished to help an economically depressed area, and when the manufacturer began publicizing the "President's House Crystal" at ten dollars a dozen, the First Lady said that she did not mind at all.

The Kennedy glassware, made by Lenox since the Morgantown firm went out of business, still appears at state dinners. It features no design or insignia (although glassware with the Seal of the United States is still used in American embassies around the world), and every White House guest who raises a toast—no matter how impressive the occasion—is drinking from an inexpensive glass indistinguishable from that used in thousands of American homes.

The democratization of the White House glassware is not echoed in its china, nor is the reliance on American workmanship. No administration before the twentieth century purchased American-made china. Francophile James Monroe bought from a French company and later Presidents followed his lead, adding to the service he had started. Julia Grant considered purchasing her countrymen's products but rejected each sample as inferior. Finally she selected a pattern made at Haviland's French factory. It featured a gold band, with the traditional presidential seal at the top and a delicate floral arrangement in the center.

The Grants' dinners broke tradition in several ways. Now that the nation had developed into a major industrial, economic, and political power, its leader could afford to vie in elegance and style with the royal houses of Europe. President and Mrs. Grant em-

The China Room on the ground floor of the White House exhibits dishes used by Presidents for nearly two centuries.

157

First Lady Lucy Hayes liked to show guests through the White House conservatory after dinner. Here she is shown with two of her children and a family friend.

ployed an Italian chef who had practiced his skills in America's most fashionable hotels, and he came well equipped to plan and execute elaborate menus. Dinners of many courses—sometimes twenty-nine—became the rule, and guests had the opportunity to try intricate concoctions never before encountered on this side of the Atlantic. One reporter described a dinner beginning with a French vegetable soup better than ever before tasted, and then "croquet of meat" and partridges. Six wineglasses and a bouquet of fresh flowers marked each place and a well-trained staff, in white starched uniforms and kid gloves, served each guest. Clearly this was a dinner meant to compete with the palaces of Europe rather than reflect the simplicity of a frontier people.

As so often happens in American history, the trend toward "royal" china was interrupted by a backlash from provincial America. Lucy Hayes, an Ohioan who lived in the White House for only four years, stamped her Midwestern print on the china collection in a remarkable way. By the 1870s it had become accepted that each administration would select a new state china, its quality and appearance being taken as a mark of the First Lady's style, and Lucy Hayes decided to order a set of plates featuring painted ferns. Theodore Davis, a young artist employed by *Harper's Weekly*, met her by chance and became friendly with her entire family, especially her son Webb. Davis suggested that Mrs. Hayes expand the fern motif to show the full variety of flora and fauna in North America. The First Lady liked the idea, and Davis labored for months over the designs. The result was a set of state china showing a good selection of the plants and animals of North America—from buckwheat to cactus to raccoons and shad—a virtual cornucopia of the continent. One White House aide later judged it "about as ugly as it is possible for china to be," but the wife of a Maine senator disagreed and argued: "It is worth a trip from New York to Washington to see the table at a state dinner at the White House." In 1975 historian Margaret Klapthor called the Hayes china a peak in the "Nationalist period" (1845–93), when the emphasis was on "American themes."

In 1889, when First Lady Caroline Harrison found that she had too few plates of any one pattern to serve a state dinner unless she used the Hayes china, she opted for something new. An accom-

A serving platter from the Hayes china.

159

plished artist, the First Lady continued the nationalist theme but in a more restrained way, working with a designer to produce a pattern that combined goldenrod and corn with the presidential seal. She had hoped to use an American company in order to underline her commitment to American workmanship, but none of the samples submitted measured up to her requirements and in the end she ordered the china from France.

Edith Roosevelt, recognizing how much interest Americans showed in the presidential china, bought special display cabinets, and Edith Wilson later designated one entire room on the ground floor for its exhibition. Eventually, the collection of White House china became one of the most popular displays at 1600 Pennsylvania Avenue. Subsequent First Ladies selected their patterns with exhibition in mind, and since 1966 an extra place setting is routinely ordered for the Smithsonian Institution.

Selecting a Lenox pattern, Edith Wilson was the first to purchase American-made china for the White House. She took her time in the matter and examined several samples made especially for her before finding one that suited her taste for color and pattern. The winning design, later reordered by the Harding, Coolidge, and Hoover administrations, makes a table about as regal as any democratic nation can condone. The plates are bordered in gold and feature the presidential seal, with the eagle clutching a laurel branch with thirteen leaves on one side and a sheaf of thirteen arrows on the other. Never known for skimping, Edith Wilson placed an order for $11,251 worth of dishes including ten dozen plates for each of the following: dinner, soup, fish, entrée, dessert, and salad. The order also included after-dinner cups as well as lesser numbers of platters and serving pieces. Marked in gold on the back of each is:

THE WHITE HOUSE
1918

Fifteen years later the nation struggled through a deep depression but newly installed First Lady Eleanor Roosevelt faced the same dilemma as several of her predecessors. Additional china had been ordered during the 1920s but not enough to compensate for breakage. When newspapers announced that Mrs. Roosevelt had requested 1,000 pieces (at a total cost of about $9,000), criticism mounted and she felt obliged to explain in one of her news conferences that it was more economical to buy an entire new service than to purchase piecemeal replacements. Her actual order was nearly twice that originally announced (1,722 pieces) and was filled, as the Wilson order had been, by Lenox.

The Roosevelt porcelain, ready for use at a dinner for ninety-nine guests honoring the heads of foreign missions on January 24, 1935, won praise from the press. More blue than gold, it acknowledged its national role by featuring the presidential seal and a band of forty-eight stars (the number of states then in the Union). But the design chosen made a personal statement as well—the narrow gold scroll inside the blue border comprised roses and three feathers, details taken from the Roosevelt family coat of arms. The back of the plate is stamped "The White House 1934."

By 1951 Bess Truman faced a perennial problem—insufficient matching dishes to serve a state dinner. When she ordered a new set, her husband, who was a history buff, saw that an old error was corrected. The presidential seal, variously drawn over the years, was now standardized. According to an executive order of October 25, 1945, the eagle would forever face the peaceful olive branch, and the words *E Pluribus Unum* would issue from its beak. To coordinate colors with the new "Williamsburg green" walls of the State Dining Room, the Truman china had a large green band. Its cost, almost three times that for which Eleanor Roosevelt had been criticized earlier, reflected the inflated prices of post-World War II America. The china was ready for use on April 3, 1952, the first time the Trumans were able to entertain in the White House after a lengthy period of renovation; their guests that day were Dutch Queen Juliana and her consort Prince Bernhard.

The Truman china, combined with pieces from sets purchased by previous administrations, served the White House for more than a decade. Then, in 1966, Lady Bird Johnson ordered a pattern designed by Tiffany featuring delicate wildflowers and the presidential seal that had by then become *de rigueur*. It was paid for by an anonymous donor and the First Lady chose not to reveal its cost.

By 1981, when the Reagans moved into the White House, the lack of suitable china again became a matter of concern. The John-

China purchased during the Lyndon Johnson administration.

Nancy Reagan ordered a china pattern that featured
the presidential seal.

son pattern seemed too casual for a state dinner, and at a dinner for King Hussein of Jordan in 1980, the Carters mixed plates from different sets in order to produce a formal look. An article in *Newsweek* complained about the indignity of combining patterns but noted that a sufficiently large new service would cost $300,000.

Nancy Reagan turned to Lenox to make a new state service, and the result featured a gold band around a red border. She applied many tests before making her final selection, including close observation under candlelight. The bill, totaling $209,508 for 4,372 pieces, reflected the general rise in prices and included no profit for Lenox, who did the job at cost. Paid for by the Knapp Foundation through the White House Historical Association, the Reagan china was ready for use on February 3, 1982, when Egyptian President Hosni Mubarak and his wife came to dine.

Although the china cost considerably less than *Newsweek* had predicted, many Americans thought the sum exorbitant, especially since it coincided with a White House announcement of cuts in public programs such as child care and school lunches. The Reagan china was retained, however, and joined its predecessors in the White House china exhibit, rounding out nearly two centuries of presidential plates.

★★★

More than a million people walk by the White House china exhibit every year, then up the wide staircase to the state floor. Proceeding like visitors to any of the nation's museums, they move along a designated path with brief stops to admire the superb portraits of the Presidents and First Ladies, the exquisitely crafted furniture and antique accessories, and the elegant serving pieces that have been used by presidential families dating back to the Madisons. Encompassing a remarkable collection of American furnishings, art, and design, the White House is not only a national landmark—it is a living museum.

HOUSE OF THE PEOPLE

★ The White House has always served as the People's House—a place to celebrate important holidays and unite at times of national mourning, a place to receive distinguished visitors and showcase the nation's talent. When tensions run high, such as at a war's beginning or conclusion, the crowds around the White House swell, but even at other times throughout the year a steady stream of Americans of all ages and backgrounds converge at 1600 Pennsylvania Avenue. Parents stand in line for hours so that their children can tour the public rooms, and people from across the country and even from abroad come to demonstrate and to make their opinions heard. Legislators on Capitol Hill might like to think that they work more closely with the people,

In June 1978 Eubie Blake, at age 95, played ragtime on the South Lawn.

but it is the President's House that draws the largest crowds, making the White House a magnet in every season.

In the first decades of the Republic, Presidents underlined the public's ownership by referring to "the People's House" and opening the residence to visitors. In the 1860s when fears for the President's safety caused the welcome mat to be retracted, the number of invitations climbed as a kind of compensation, and crowds continued to congregate outside the gates as if the White House were a town square or public hall. In the twentieth century, when the population grew too large and the distances too great for most Americans to make their way to 1600 Pennsylvania Avenue, television took the building to them, and they were invited to watch their President speak from the Oval Office and listen to celebrities "In Performance at the White House."

Unlike the homes of other world leaders, the President's House is open year-round for public viewing. Many visitors share the sentiment of the youngster who, when reprimanded for jumping on a sofa at Andrew Jackson's inauguration party, replied defiantly, "It is one-millionth part mine."

White House residents have publicly acknowledged the American people's proprietary interest. When Eleanor Roosevelt moved into the White House during the Great Depression, she explained she did so with a heavy heart; no woman could do otherwise, she noted, if "she accepts the fact that it belongs to the people and therefore must be representative of whatever conditions people are facing." Lady Bird Johnson echoed those feelings when she called the White House a "rich storehouse of recollections" not just to Presidents but to the "whole nation."

More than any other dwelling in the United States, the White House arouses curiosity—people want to know about the foods served, the exercise taken, the pets kept, and the music played. When the purchases appear excessive, Americans complain of "royal" trappings—but then they object at least as loudly if the President and First Lady settle for out-of-style clothing or less than elegant dining. Although it is strictly forbidden, visitors during a tour have been known to run their fingers over a windowsill to check its cleanliness. Others comment on the height at which the grass is cut—as though this were their own backyard.

★★★

Even before its plaster had dried, back on January 1, 1801, the President's House opened its doors to the public. The tradition had already been established by George Washington that the nation's Chief Executive would receive callers on the first day of the year. Aware of the value of appearing close to his constituents, Washington had immediately announced upon taking office in 1789 that he would entertain at two weekly parties at his home throughout the year: Men would visit him on Tuesday afternoons at a levée (or reception) and all were welcome with their wives at Martha Washington's party on Friday evening.

That very first year of his presidency, the levée happened to fall on January 1, and George Washington decided, in an act of generosity or an attempt to win public approval, to open his home to everyone. Each guest would be greeted by the President of the United States and his wife, drink a cup of punch, and mix with the others present. In eighteenth-century America an open house of this sort was common on New Year's Day—some employers invited their workers to come by for a toast to the future, and apprentices were permitted to enter homes closed to them the other 364 days of the year. But for heads of state, such parties were rare.

Not everyone in New York City, the nation's temporary capital, was inclined to call on the Washingtons. Ideas about deference and propriety kept many of the poor away from their leader's house. Even in the aftermath of the Revolution, Americans could not shed some old traditions, nor could they break accepted rules about who called on whom. A liveryman or an apprentice shoemaker who did not work for the President would not have ventured into his house. If asked why, he would have been surprised by the question. He had never voted, nor did he expect to, and he felt little inclination to approach the President. His wife might have been curious about the interior of the President's House but would have been too uncomfortable with the idea of entering it to venture through the front door.

Fashionable New Yorkers who put themselves on a social par with the President were not so reticent and welcomed the opportunity to see how the Washingtons entertained. When one of the women guests judged the cream in the dessert trifle a bit rancid, word spread that Lady Washington had a few things to learn.

Philadelphians proved just as curious, and when the federal government moved to the City of Brotherly Love in 1791, they lined up for the New Year's Day reception. Eleven of these receptions occurred prior to November 1800, when John and Abigail Adams moved to Washington, and the Adamses felt they could do no less than open the doors of the President's House to the public on January 1.

Washington City, as it was called then, had fewer than five hundred households, so the turnout was only a fraction of what it would later become. The oval room on the second floor was made as presentable as possible and, to add a festive note, the President and First Lady invited the Marine Band to play, making it the first

As part of her First Lady duties, Jacqueline Kennedy welcomed many visitors to the White House.

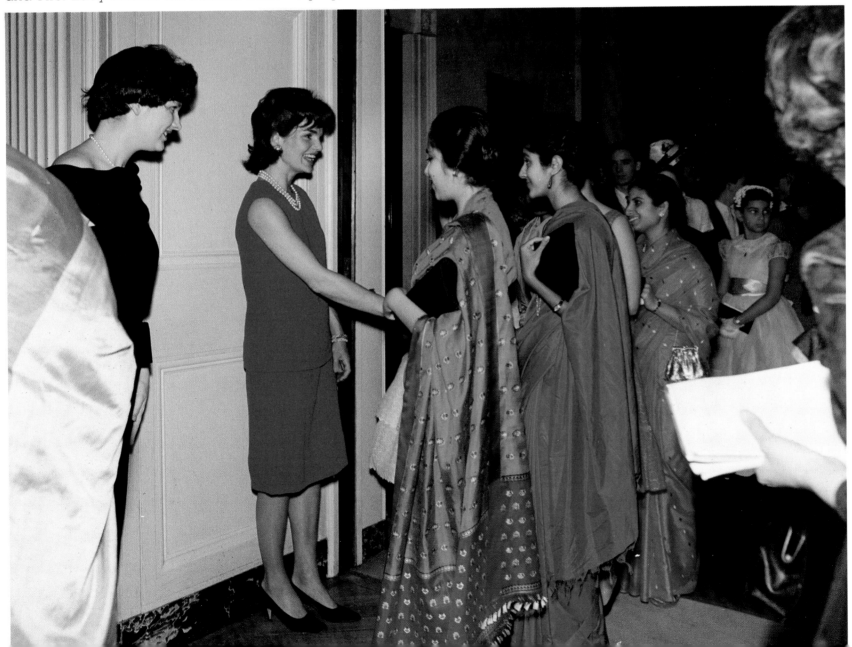

musical group to perform in the White House. Forming a tiny ensemble of two French horns, two clarinets, and a bassoon, the bandsmen, in red jackets and blue pantaloons, provided the brightest color in the room. They could not know, nor could the guests as they filed upstairs to greet John and Abigail Adams, that they were initiating a tradition that would last, with some interruptions, for 132 years—without invitation, anyone could visit the President's House on New Year's Day.

The following year (1802), Thomas Jefferson continued the tradition of inviting in the public to celebrate on January 1. Although the refreshment served was a bit unorthodox, it appropriately carried strong partisan overtones at a time when political parties were still taking shape. Jefferson's Republican admirers in West Chester, Pennsylvania, had sent him a wagon drawn by six horses and carrying a 1,235-pound cheese that they claimed was made from the milk of "Republican" cows. New Year's guests, more heavily Republican that year than previously, ate with particular

Rosalynn Carter poses with a group of Girl Scouts in the State Dining Room.

gusto, pleased that they controlled the presidency—the ultimate "big cheese."

In the summer of 1801, during his first year as President, Thomas Jefferson decided to open the lawn around the President's House in celebration of the day independence was declared. He arranged for a large party on July 4, and the event quickly became the best attended of the year. Whether the Chief Executive was in residence or not, people flocked to his house for the festivities. The tradition would continue into the twentieth century, and when the grounds were eventually closed off, people expected fireworks on the Mall or concerts at the Capitol building to supplement their celebration.

In addition to the January 1 and July 4 holidays, the White House opened for smaller groups of visitors at other times. Thomas Jefferson permitted public tours, and Dolley Madison, a First Lady who combined an unusually large measure of political savvy with the sure hand of a seasoned hostess, followed his lead. She recognized the political value of being popular, and every Wednesday evening between six and nine anyone could visit the Madisons at home. Technically, only those who had been introduced to the President and his wife (or knew someone who had been) were invited, but that was a latitude easily stretched, and on the designated day "Open House" prevailed.

A wide range of people accepted. When author Washington Irving visited the capital in 1811, he "swore by all my gods" that he would attend one of Dolley Madison's parties. So did hundreds of clerks and congressmen's relatives. The First Lady moved among them all, greeting strangers warmly and conversing with her husband's enemies as much as with his friends. President Madison, brilliant with a pen but a failure at party talk, stayed on the sidelines, willing to respond to those who sought him out but never comfortable as a host.

Massachusetts congressman Elijah Mills, a political opponent of Madison's, complained that the drawing rooms were "full of intrigue, political and moral" and the guests were not those he would have chosen: "all classes of people are there from men from Russia to underclerks of the Post Office and the printer of a paper—greasy boots and silk stockings"—and many of the women showed "very much the manners and appearances of 'high life below the stairs.'"

To speed the flow of traffic, this bridge was built so that guests could exit directly from the East Room to the lawn. *Frank Leslie's Illustrated Newspaper,* March 16, 1889.

Crowding was common, and one woman who attended an 1814 reception at the Executive Mansion described how people had to "compress themselves as small as they could" in order for everyone to get inside. Unfortunately, in their zeal they caused some damage, and "in the excessive heat of the apartments, the rouge, which had been applied with 'an unsparing hand' began to run together with powder, dust and perspiration, making their wearers 'altogether unlovely to soul and eye.'"

As the nation grew and the capital city expanded, the crowds multiplied. Lines of three or four abreast formed outside the Executive Mansion, curling down the hill as people waited to shake hands with the President. Eventually a temporary bridge was added from the East Room to the lawn so guests could exit directly rather than wind around through the house again, clogging the traffic flow.

New Year's Day 1818 was an especially important celebration, since that day had been selected for reopening the President's House after its 1814 burning. Workmen rushed to meet the deadline, and curious Americans lined up to see the results. One congressman estimated that a thousand people appeared that day, but President James Monroe and his wife Elizabeth stood through the ordeal of greeting each one, "nodding, bowing, smiling and talking. . . . The fatigue must have been very great."

For the diplomatic corps and the congressmen (who, beginning in 1818, were admitted ahead of the general public), an appearance at the President's House on January 1 became practically obligatory. A newspaper editor's wife thought attendance was "generally deemed a test of loyalty" no matter what the weather. Torrents of rain came down on New Year's Day 1823, but a New England congressman reported that virtually everyone he knew went to "the palace." Louisa Adams, wife of John Quincy Adams, then Secretary of State, noted in her diary that she had attended the President's reception although she was "miserably sick."

Americans looked for other chances during the year to visit the White House, and they were often obliged by Presidents who realized the advantages of remaining accessible. Andrew Jackson chose Washington's birthday to give the last public reception of his presidency (in February 1837) and he offered as refreshment a "mammoth cheese" (weighing 1400 pounds) that had come as a gift from admiring farmers in Oswego County, New York. According to some who were present that day, the smell of cheese filled the entire house and went beyond, reaching the Capitol building where congressmen, after filling their pockets with cheese, had gone to work.

Andrew Jackson became famous for attracting huge crowds wherever he went. For his first inauguration in 1829 so many people descended on the capital that room-and-board prices soared, and one report had a dozen eggs selling for eighty cents, more than most working people earned in a day. After Jackson's inaugural ceremony the crowd at the President's House surpassed all previous gatherings, a fact that was noted with some displeasure in newspaper accounts of the day. Supreme Court Justice Joseph Story fled the scene, saying that he wanted to avoid a mixture of

Supporters of Andrew Jackson sent him a mammoth cheese which he served at a White House reception.

people ranging "from the highest and most polished down to the most vulgar in the nation."

A Pennsylvania congressman who was present that day described a White House so crowded that waiters could not serve the barrels of orange punch they had prepared. People rushed the doors, "glasses were broken, pails of liquor upset and the most painful confusion prevailed." The congressman claimed to have seen men and boys, "boots heavy with mud," standing on satin damask-covered chairs. Not until waiters carried the punch out onto the White House lawn did the crowd inside begin to thin out.

Presidents dared not offend voters by closing the White House gates too abruptly. When President Martin Van Buren, who had a reputation for fancy manners and high living, tried to dispense with the Fourth of July party in 1839, he was loudly criticized. Presidents soon learned that if they wished to flee hot, humid Washington in July, they should arrange for the celebration to proceed without them. Even President Polk, reputedly a workaholic, took time to visit with callers, and twice a month he and his wife Sarah gave a reception following the Marine Band concerts. As many as two hundred people showed up.

Carriages lined up outside the North Portico, the principal public entrance during the nineteenth century.

Union soldiers camped in the East Room during the Civil War.

By the 1860s, this kind of open house seemed inappropriate and Mary Lincoln tried to put a stop to it. The city had grown, bringing many more people into visiting proximity. The mood in Washington was bitter, with the nation divided in a Civil War. President Lincoln wanted to hold the receptions even in wartime, and he continued to schedule them, but he feared for his own safety and that of his family. Anxiety ran so high, President Lincoln's private secretary William Osborn Stoddard wrote, that Mary Lincoln asked him to open every letter and parcel addressed to her.

The large number of invitation cards that she issued—as many as five hundred for a single event—suggests that Mary Lincoln went beyond inviting just the capital elite. Those honored with a card were expected to show it at the door, go up to the second floor to deposit coats and hats, and then return to one of the state rooms on the main floor (often the Blue Room) to be greeted by the President and First Lady. All evening the Marine Band supplied "sweet music" in the background, and about 11 P.M. a procession led by the Lincolns moved down the grand hallway to the dining room, where

Regardless of cold weather and snow, people lined up for blocks to greet the President and his wife on New Year's Day.

a table provided "one of the finest displays of the confectioner's art ever seen in this country."

Some criticism greeted this kind of restricted, invitation-only affair and critics used it as ammunition in their crusade against Mary Lincoln, but in the end it was accepted as necessitated by circumstances. Anyone with even a little clout or minimal acquaintance could arrange for a place on one of the guest lists, but the right to attend on whim—except on January 1—was taken away.

Popular First Lady Frances Cleveland greeted an exceptionally long line of visitors on New Year's Day 1887. Just months earlier, she had become the first to marry a President in the White House. Only twenty-two years old at the time, she created a sensation and her picture appeared in magazines across the country. A nineteenth-century version of Jacqueline Kennedy, "Frankie" Cleveland was imitated in dress and hairstyle by thousands of women. People willingly stood in line for hours on New Year's Day just to shake her hand, and some reportedly claimed the privilege more than once. The First Lady obligingly greeted each one, but to ease the strain she had to resort to brief massages of her hands and arms.

First Lady Edith Roosevelt clutched a bouquet of orchids to avoid shaking hands. That ruse was insufficient, however, to keep people in line moving quickly, and the Marine Band conductor developed another strategy to influence the flow of traffic. After starting with slow, soft pieces, orchestrated without drums or cymbals, he introduced a little light opera music as diplomats and congressmen filed past; then as the general public was admitted and the crowds grew, the band played loud marches. The President and his wife reported that they saw a change—people seemed to flow with the music, moving faster when it was faster, thus permitting more of them to be greeted in less time and leaving the hosts less fatigued at the end of the day.

Unfortunately there were pranksters, and some of them were dangerous. Fear escalated after President McKinley was shot while greeting the public in 1901. The assassination took place in Buffalo while the President attended the Pan-American Exposition, but the effect back in Washington was direct and immediate. McKinley's successor, Theodore Roosevelt, announced a new rule: no one— not even a close friend—could go through the receiving line and

Although Americans allow their Presidents some latitude in decorating the White House, one cartoonist implied that Theodore Roosevelt had gone too far with his wild game theme.

approach the President while carrying a muff or bundle of any kind.

The Roosevelt rule had little effect on two men intent on playing a practical joke at a New Year's Day reception. From the front they appeared appropriately dressed, but from the back they were walking billboards: the placards attached to their jackets promoted a well-known mineral water. The President was not amused and amended his rules so that only those who were "clean and free of bodily advertising" were to be admitted.

During Theodore Roosevelt's second term, between 5,000 and 9,000 people filed through the White House every New Year's, and an extra aide was assigned to stand opposite the President to watch for dangerous people. Security men were rotated so as to encourage vigilance.

Occasionally the receptions had to be canceled because of a national emergency, illness, or extenuating circumstance, but the decision was not made lightly. Of course none could be held immediately after the 1814 burning of the President's House, and Benjamin Harrison had to call off the party in 1893 after his granddaughter, Marthena Harrison, was quarantined with scarlet fever. The child was confined to two rooms on the northwest corner of the second floor, but prudence dictated keeping crowds away from the entire mansion. Harrison's presidency must have seemed jinxed by then; his wife had died the previous October, and he had lost his November bid for reelection.

The cancellation of the New Year's White House reception by the Harrisons was noted by Woodrow Wilson in 1915 when he, too, considered calling it off. His wife had died only five months previously and the Great War had already started in Europe. Celebration was hardly the feeling of the day. Even then Wilson hesitated, not willing to risk being called "elitist." Finally he was persuaded, one of his secretaries reported, by the Harrison precedent. Word went out that the President would not be greeting visitors that day.

Not everyone in Washington looked forward to the January 1 reception. Diplomats and congressional representatives had other opportunities to see the interior of the White House, and many of the capital's elite attended various dinners and receptions during the year. Janet Richards, a lecturer and suffrage leader, received invitations to White House parties over five decades, beginning with the McKinley administration in 1897, and she explained to her friends that she had more interesting things to do on January 1 than mix with the masses and shake hands with the President.

In 1932 when bad weather deterred many people from standing in line to greet the Hoovers, Richards noted in her diary that it had been an altogether miserable day—a "pouring down rainy day! Such a disappointment to the thousands who had planned to storm the White House . . . for their one annual 'look in' on the . . . great."

The poor turnout in 1932, added to the disenchantment of Washington officials and the President's own disappointment with the continuing economic depression, combined to put a stop to the New Year's receptions. By January 1933, Herbert Hoover had presided over a depression-torn country for nearly four years, and when he had run for reelection the previous November he had lost. Hardly in the mood for a party, Hoover had no reason to think other people were, and considering his unpopularity, the number of callers might have been embarrassingly small. During the last four-month interval between the presidential election and inauguration (beginning in 1937, Presidents would take the oath on January 20 rather than on March 4), the Hoovers decided to take off for a much-needed rest in the South rather than stay around Washington to shake hands.

The President's New Year's reception was not revived again, and the long line of Americans shaking hands with their President on January 1 became a thing of the past. Invitations would now become the rule for all White House events, although tourists would still be permitted to walk through the state rooms during designated hours.

The number of names on guest lists soared in order to compensate for the decreased accessibility. Each year thousands of average citizens received cards admitting them to garden parties, receptions, luncheons, and teas—their names carefully typed and indexed in the White House social records prepared by the staff. Edith Helm, secretary to Eleanor Roosevelt, noted that during the 1935–36 season more than 27,000 people accepted an invitation to the White House: 906 for lunch, 1099 for dinner, 5672 for state

New Year's Day receptions drew large crowds for more than a century.

receptions, and 19,713 for tea. The presidential family shared quarters with 378 overnight guests, and sightseers walked through the state rooms at the rate of more than 70,000 per month.

Music was often a central feature of White House parties, and after its very first appearance in 1801 the Marine Band became a regular attraction at all but the smallest, most casual events. Bands of other military branches would eventually rotate in the White House performance schedule but the Marine Band was most closely associated with the Chief Executive and became known as the "President's own."

In the 1840s the Marine Band began regular concerts on the White House lawn, and these free events attracted a loyal following. Frederika Bremer, a Swedish visitor to the capital in early July 1850, reported what she had observed when she attended. People sat on the grass, munched picnic lunches, and strolled about, greeting their friends and stopping, if they chose, to chat with the President. Zachary Taylor, the military hero who had reluctantly assumed the presidency, evidently enjoyed this part of the job, and one visitor noted that he was always ready to "shake hands with anyone who chooses to present himself."

Eventually the band concerts were shifted temporarily to Wednesdays because First Lady Jane Pierce insisted on tranquillity as she prepared for religious services on Sundays, but she dared not stop the music. People expected the lawn to be open to them, and they took it as their right to use it without any special invitation.

The intrepid Mary Lincoln asked that the concerts be stopped after her son Willie died in 1862, but she was loudly criticized. The music and laughter grated on her nerves, she said, at a time when her life was so full of grief. Abraham Lincoln liked listening to the music but objected to the attention he attracted whenever he appeared. The President had stepped out on the South Portico one Saturday afternoon to hear the band better, but as soon as the audience caught sight of his tall, gaunt figure, they requested a speech. He immediately retreated, remarking to a friend, "I wish they would let me sit out there quietly and enjoy the music."

The band's membership remained largely foreign—mostly Germans and Italians—throughout the nineteenth century because the United States had not yet developed many of its own music

181

Maestro Dino Anagnost (second from left) paused for this photo on the South Lawn after conducting the New York Metropolitan Singers/Greek Choral Society in a concert in the East Room. The concert and reception honored his Eminence Archbishop Iakovos, Primate of the Greek Orthodox Church in the Americas (on the left).

schools. Nor did it have a sufficiently large number of musicians to apprentice younger ones. Until 1880 foreigners conducted the Marine Band, when American-born John Philip Sousa took over. With an emphasis on patriotic themes in his music, Sousa composed more than one hundred marches including such classics as "Semper Fidelis," "Stars and Stripes Forever," and the "Washington Post March."

Musical entertainment had been popular inside the President's House from the very beginning. Thomas Jefferson, an accomplished violinist himself, arranged for music at his receptions, and he personally owned several keyboard instruments. Louisa Adams kept her harp and sheet music handy, and the newly wed John and Julia Tyler teamed up for duets.

These musical programs remained private until the middle of the nineteenth century when the mansion began receiving world-famous artists. Adelina Patti, one of the most sought-after sopranos of the late 1800s, came to visit the President but she did not sing. Perhaps she had qualms about performing without being paid, since she was used to receiving five thousand dollars for such appearances. The tradition of performing for free, however, still continues into the White House's third century. An artist invited to entertain at the White House receives a plaque or a signed photo— perhaps even a dinner and a chance to stay overnight—but not a check from the President.

Rutherford Hayes deserves credit for introducing "musicales" at the White House, and during his four years as President he scheduled fifty such events, combining a private concert with a chance to socialize. One featured Maria Selika, the first African-American to sing at the White House. Chester Arthur arranged for the first concert in the East Room, and during Theodore Roosevelt's administration the White House blossomed with music. Hundreds of people came to hear world figures such as pianist Ignace Paderewski, who first performed in the East Room in 1902. He returned to play nine times for seven different Presidents, eventually bringing his own piano with him so he could practice in the Queens' Bedroom (where he also slept).

Regardless of personal preferences, each presidential family tries to invite performers and present compositions popular with the

American people. In 1905 the Marine Band learned Scott Joplin's "Maple Leaf Rag" in response to pressure from Theodore Roosevelt's family; Mamie Eisenhower scheduled the bands of Lawrence Welk and Fred Waring in the 1950s; in the early 1960s the Kennedys presented the legendary cellist Pablo Casals (who had first performed at the White House in 1904); and ten years later the Nixons invited country-western singer Johnny Cash.

Struggling artists profit from the boost of a White House appearance and marginal figures move into the mainstream. First Lady Helen Taft, an accomplished pianist herself, favored keyboard music in making up her concert list, and nine of the eleven pianists that she invited to the White House were women. In 1935 Eleanor Roosevelt's invitation to Antonia Brico. to conduct the New York Women's Symphony in a concert of Mozart selections came at a time when women musicians were rare and women conductors even more so. Brico's career was just beginning and the White House appearance paved the way for her to conduct later at major concert halls in the United States and Europe. In 1962 Grace Bumbry was still an unknown opera singer when she appeared in the East Room, but her career soared after just one performance at the Kennedy White House.

Before the Kennedy Center for the Performing Arts opened in 1971, the White House frequently functioned as a theater, presenting such shows as *Hello Dolly*, whose cast gathered to celebrate its fourth anniversary on January 17, 1967.

In December 1990, Barbara Bush showed visitors the Christmas tree in the Blue Room.

One of President Bush's granddaughters joins him with a basket of Easter eggs in the Oval Office.

By the end of its second century, the White House had been the setting for just about every variety of musical performance— ranging from the Beach Boys to Isaac Stern (who played the violin for seven Presidents). The jazz group that had shocked Lou Hoover's guests at a Christmas party for her son would now no longer create a stir, and when the Carters arranged for televising the programs, the audience for "In Performance at the White House" became potentially almost as large as the nation itself. Rosalynn Carter explained that the idea of televising musical performances resulted from the realization that "so many people who had never been to the White House would be thrilled to come."

Although musicians have most often been the featured performers at White House programs, other entertainers have also appeared, including dancers, monologists, and theatrical groups. Before Kennedy Center opened in 1971, the White House functioned as a leading theater for professional readings of Shakespeare, ballet performances, and Broadway shows.

★ ★ ★

Just as Americans have gathered at the President's House for various performances, they have also come to it for holiday celebrations. First Lady Nancy Reagan recalled that as a child she had rolled Easter eggs on the South Lawn, a tradition that Lucy Hayes is credited with beginning. Children of employees or friends of the Chief Executive eagerly anticipated the annual lawn party, and the numbers attending were particularly large if the President had young children.

In 1885, an oversight resulted in no preparations being made for the party, but when bachelor President Cleveland heard of the mistake, he immediately ordered the grounds opened for all to enjoy. Thousands arrived, carrying colored eggs they meant to roll and exchange before settling down to picnic lunches. Thirsty crowds converged on the mansion, and President Cleveland sent word that he would greet them in the East Room. He had not foreseen how many would take advantage of the offer and finally he was advised to retreat—otherwise he would have been shaking youngsters' hands until dark.

The Easter egg roll continued to draw ever increasing numbers. In April 1961, an estimated ten thousand people converged

184

on the White House lawn even though the Kennedys had gone to Florida. In the absence of the presidential family, the Air Force Band played and the city's recreation department organized games. Even this gigantic turnout did not break the record set in 1941 when an estimated 53,248 people showed up.

That same year marked an unusual Christmas tree lighting. Since the 1890s, White House families had put a Christmas tree inside the mansion and, since 1923, another tree outside. Placement of the exterior tree varied—sometimes it was on the Ellipse (south of the White House) or in Lafayette Park (to the north). But whatever the location, the tree drew large crowds and its brilliant colored lights added to the city's Christmas festivities.

In 1941 the Secret Service protested. Civil Defense precautions blacked out the city at night, and protection of the President (and Winston Churchill, who happened to be a guest) required that the White House not be targeted by anything so prominent as a lit Christmas tree. President Roosevelt objected that he would not be denied his tree, and by means of compromise the community tree was moved to the South Lawn—within the fenced White House grounds so the President could be more closely protected.

Christmas Eve 1941 turned out to be a particularly mild winter

In November 1918, when word spread through the capital that World War I was finally over, crowds gathered at the White House.

night, and thousands of men and women gathered to sing carols and hear short speeches by Franklin Roosevelt and Winston Churchill, the first meeting of a President and British Prime Minister on Christmas Eve. The men spoke from the South Portico while other distinguished guests, including the Crown Prince and Princess of Norway, stood behind them. Then the President pushed a button and the giant tree was lit, thus beginning the tradition of a "national" Christmas tree near the President's House.

Crowds have gathered many times on that same lawn to celebrate military victory. The President may actually sign the peace document inside the White House—as William McKinley did in 1898 when he went to a second floor room (now known as the Treaty Room) and put his name on the document that ended the Spanish-American War—but the real signature belongs to the people shouting outside. In November 1918, throngs of Americans gathered near the White House gates. Actually they gathered too soon, having heard a false report that the Great War was already over four days before it actually was. They had to be sent away, Edith Wilson explained, but then on Monday November 11, they returned, and this time their shouts were justified. Jubilant crowds also gathered to celebrate V-E day and V-J day in 1945 at the end of World War II.

Not all Americans come to the White House in celebration— some come in anger, frustration or concern, as they would to a community meeting house. Then Lafayette Park becomes a mass of signs announcing opinions and demanding action. South of the White House, the Ellipse can become packed, a sea of angry voices reaching up to the President's office and to his bedroom.

No one can be sure what single protester deserves credit for first taking his case directly to the President in a public way, but John Tyler came up against more than one of them. Tyler's presidency began inauspiciously in April 1841, when he became the first Vice President to take over after the death of an incumbent, William Henry Harrison. Tyler alienated the Whig party leaders by insisting on being granted full discretionary powers as President and by vetoing a fiscal bill drawn up by the Whigs. After a few drinks at local saloons, an ugly mob moved toward the Executive Mansion. Finding the gates closed, they began screaming, throw-

On a wet, snow-covered lawn, Americans gathered in January 1945 to witness an unprecedented fourth inauguration for Franklin D. Roosevelt as President.

ing rocks, and firing guns. A particularly irate group took up space right across the street and burned the President in effigy—surely a frightening sight for the Tyler family inside a relatively unguarded house.

Unanimity is rare in a democratic society where the Constitution ensures the right to freedom of speech, and the White House continues to serve as a focal point for differing ideas. In the 1960s Lafayette Park became a permanent protest ground, providing the space for thousands of demonstrators to make their opinions known directly to the President. The family of Lyndon Johnson endured twenty-four-hour-a-day chanting, and his daughters, whose husbands were serving in Vietnam, could not help but be distressed by shouts of anti-war demonstrators: "LBJ/ LBJ/ How many boys/ did you kill today?" The Nixons learned to eat lunch inside the White

Suffragists converged on the White House in 1917 to gain President Woodrow Wilson's support for women's voting rights.

PRESIDENT WILSON IS DECEIVING THE WORLD WHEN HE APPEARS AS THE PROPHET OF DEMOCRACY

PRESIDENT WILSON HAS OPPOSED THOSE WHO DEMAND DEMOCRACY FOR THIS COUNTRY

HE IS RESPONSIBLE FOR THE DISFRANCHISEMENT OF MILLIONS OF AMERICANS

WE IN AMERICA KNOW THIS THE WORLD WILL FIND HIM OUT.

House, the unmistakable smell of tear gas wafting up to them.

Betty Ford, after publicly supporting the Equal Rights Amendment to bar discrimination on the basis of sex, suffered the indignity of seeing her views disparaged in the park in front of the White House. Then, on the televised evening news, she saw a replay—black-clad figures parading through the park carrying placards denouncing her for pressing "second-rate manhood on American women."

All important national questions get debated on White House space, or as close to it as proponents of different views are permitted to come. Sometimes that seems very close. In the fall of 1990, when the United States and its allies considered how to move Iraqi soldiers out of Kuwait, Lafayette Park filled with people and signs opposing military action. Their numbers grew, and in January 1991, when President Bush went on television to announce that air attacks were beginning on Iraqi forces, he spoke above the shouts of protesters outside.

Like London's Hyde Park, the area outside the White House fence offers a remarkable platform. It charges no rent and guarantees immediate press coverage—reasons enough to make it a favorite site of protest. Young men and women often make a White House demonstration the reason for their first trip to Washington, and the President's House remains their strongest memory.

Sometimes the demonstrations appear to get quick results. In early 1917 advocates of the vote for women, convinced that Woodrow Wilson's failure to support a national amendment had stymied their progress, converged on the White House. Some of the suffragists chained themselves to the gates and others were dragged away. But their signs made their point, and the President shifted his position and came out for a suffrage amendment in early 1918.

President Wilson considered the suffragist demonstrators of little danger to him personally; he even invited them in for tea—and could not understand why they declined. Each day as he went out for his afternoon ride, he tipped his hat to them in a courtly gesture that infuriated them.

Presidents have not always viewed the demonstrators so benignly. Previous Chief Executives, going as far back as Madison, put security guards on the grounds in order to protect their own

When Abraham Lincoln's body lay in state in the East Room, poor lighting precluded photographs, but an artist made this sketch so that Americans across the nation could participate vicariously in rites for their martyred President.

safety and that of their family. Gradually, and almost imperceptibly, the President's House would change into the barricaded, highly guarded and less accessible White House that Americans would come to know in the 1990s. Protection for the leader from the people stood as the very antithesis of what democracy was supposed to be about. A representative of the people should have no reason to fear, popular reasoning went, as long as he remained responsive to constituents' needs and wishes. Only in the face of attempted assassinations and increased fear did the cement barriers and a sophisticated security force come into use.

★ ★ ★

In the initial discussions of security in the early nineteenth century, the word "guard" rarely appears, and the first hired were called "watch" men as though they were merely keeping a ship on course or attending to fires that might go out. Even when John Tyler persuaded a reluctant Congress to pay for a permanent security force in the 1840s, only four men were hired and they were called "doormen." To the uninformed, they appeared to be more social fixtures than security measures as they stood around nonchalantly and mingled with guests at receptions.

In 1853 Franklin Pierce, a Democrat from New Hampshire, became the first President to have a full-time bodyguard. He had made the South Lawn into a park and hired two men to guard it at night, but he wanted reinforcements closer at hand. Having witnessed violence more than once, he was not inclined to put himself at risk. He had seen the assassination attempt on President Jackson in 1835 and had lost a close friend in a duel waged over politics. Pierce may have felt particularly vulnerable, having lost all three of his sons before any reached maturity.

Whatever his reasons, Pierce asked Thomas O'Neil, who had been his orderly in the Mexican-American War, to attend to his safety. O'Neil escorted the President down the capital's streets and went riding with him. When Pierce worked inside the White House, O'Neil ensconced himself in the entrance hall where he observed everyone who came through and, if necessary, could respond to calls for help.

A combination of events contributed to increased security measures. Abraham Lincoln's assassination in 1865 (the first of a

After President Garfield's death in 1881, the White House was draped in mourning.

After President Garfield was shot in 1881, well-wishers converged on the White House. *Frank Leslie's Illustrated Newspaper,* July 30, 1881, showed a young African-American girl presenting a bouquet of flowers.

Florence Harding greeted tourists and posed with delegations, including this group of Masons.

President) and James Garfield's in 1881 both occurred outside the Executive Mansion, but they resulted in many discussions about how to protect the President. Whenever the United States went to war, the need for extra vigilance was obvious. By the 1980s terrorist attacks around the world resulted in closing off the entire avenue east of the White House. A new visitors' entrance was built to screen everyone who passed through. At first glance, the visitors' entryway blends so well with the Palladian lines of the original mansion that it might seem part of it—but in function it is nearly two centuries removed. Its metal detectors, like those in most airports, check thousands of people every day, and guards personally inspect handbags and identification cards.

Breaches sometimes occur. White House security forces were shaken in January 1985 when a Denver man, vacationing in the capital, infiltrated the Marine Band and got up to the State Floor of the White House where he poked around for about ten minutes before the guards noticed him. Jailed for five days, he was ordered to undergo a psychiatric examination—but not before the entire building was checked for hidden explosives.

Such precautions would have shocked early nineteenth-century Americans who claimed the right to walk into the White House at any hour of the day—at least as far as the East Room. During the presidencies of Jefferson and Madison, visitors could wander in at will, and although the elusive Monroes liked their privacy and tried to keep people out, their successors opened the doors again. President Andrew Johnson announced that the East Room would be open for visitors every day except Sunday between 9 A.M. and 3 P.M. Guests could enter the north door, walk through the wide hall, and stand in the East Room for as long as they liked. Some even brought along a minister and exchanged vows so they could boast that they had been "married at the White House."

Subsequent administrations restricted access but Florence Harding brought back some of the nineteenth-century openness when she reintroduced public tours. Although self-centered in many respects, she seemed intent on making every visitor feel welcome, and staff recalled that she would frequently go downstairs from the living quarters to shake hands with tourists and have her photograph taken with whatever delegation wanted to pose.

Even after security precautions transformed the White House

into a barricaded fortress, White House residents sought ways to stay physically close to the public. Lyndon Johnson could be seen reaching through the iron fence to shake hands with tourists; Rosalynn Carter made frequent trips to the ground floor to be photographed with one delegation or another, referring to each of these picture sessions as a "bottom-of-the-elevator"; and George Bush often detoured to surprise visitors with a personal greeting.

★ ★ ★

Although it would seem that royal figures might find no welcome mat in the "People's House," in fact they have been popular guests. In 1860 the visit of the Prince of Wales (later to become King

A women's sorority posed with Florence Harding (fifth from right) on the White House portico.

Edward VII) resulted in what White House historian William Seale called a "public spectacle."

Monarchs' visits continued to dot American history in the following decades, but none aroused quite the interest accorded King George VI and Queen Elizabeth in 1939. Never before had a reigning British monarch favored the United States with a stopover, and the White House went through months of cleaning and refurbishing in preparation. In her weekly news conferences, Eleanor Roosevelt was besieged with questions on how she would accommodate her royal guests, feed them, and dress for them—and whether they merited a curtsy. Reporters felt obligated to assure readers that the nation's most visible guest house was being properly run.

For most royal visitors of the late twentieth century, the White House is simply too small to accommodate them and their entourage overnight, so they are housed across the street at the official guest quarters in Blair House. But one second-floor bedroom of the White House did earn the name of "Queens' Bedroom" in honor of the five who had stayed there. Decorated in rosy pink, this was the room Mamie Eisenhower chose as her own when she returned to visit the Nixons.

The same room also appealed to the entertainer Sammy Davis, Jr, when he was an overnight guest of the Nixons. He had been shown first to the coveted Lincoln Bedroom but had demurred,

When Britain's reigning monarchs made their historic visit to Washington in June 1939, Eleanor Roosevelt accompanied Queen Elizabeth on the ride from the train station to the White House.

The Queens' Bedroom takes its name from the fact
that many royal guests have slept there.

The domestic staff in 1877 included one cook,
two waiters, a house maid, a messenger, a watchman,
two laundresses, and a nurse.

joking later, "I thought to myself, now I don't want [Lincoln] coming in here talking about 'I freed them, but I sure didn't mean for them to sleep in my bed.' "

Davis touched on a delicate subject. Eighty percent of the domestic staff was black at the time of his visit and large numbers of African-Americans had worked in the residence since it was first occupied, their records inevitably tied to the house's history. Thomas Jefferson installed several of his Monticello slaves there, and one of them gave birth to a baby—who died less than two years later, resulting in what historians think is the first funeral held in the White House. Other Southern Presidents, notably Madison, Jackson, Polk, and Taylor, used their own personal slaves as part of the domestic staff, in an attempt to cut expenses paid out of their own pockets.

Guest status came more slowly. A small number of African-Americans joined the July 4 celebration on the White House lawn in 1864, and even more attended a reception in the Blue Room the following New Year's at which President Lincoln shook hands with all his guests. A few years later, when Julia Grant was asked if all races were welcome at her receptions she avoided the issue, saying that she expected only whites would care to attend.

Very few prominent African-Americans were entertained at the White House in the late nineteenth century, and their appearance, if publicized, did not always meet with public approval. The one-time abolitionist who later became Minister to Haiti, Frederick Douglass, accepted—without incident—a blanket invitation extended to all Washington, D.C., officials to attend a reception after Grover Cleveland's second inauguration in 1893. A few years later, in 1901, Theodore Roosevelt invited educator Booker T. Washington to dinner at the White House but found himself chastised in newspapers throughout the South. No one seemed to care that the President's sister, Corinne Robinson, invited the same guest to lunch at her New York apartment a few weeks later; she did not live in the People's House.

Public opinion had not changed much by 1929 when Lou Hoover invited Jessie DePriest, spouse of the first African-American to be elected to Congress in twenty-nine years, to a tea that the First Lady regularly gave for congressmen's wives. Some white Southerners were outraged, and several newspapers published editorials

Pat Nixon welcomes children to the East Room.

insisting that the First Lady had "defiled" the Executive Mansion.

Finally in the 1930s, groups that had formerly been barred began slowly to achieve guest status without incident, and in the following decades their numbers grew. When the Nixons paid tribute to jazz musician and composer Duke Ellington, one journalist noted that more African-Americans were present than at any previous time in the nation's history.

Gradually the White House welcome mat has extended to people of diverse ethnic backgrounds. Italian-Americans, whose countrymen had provided musical entertainment for decades, began receiving invitations to come as guests in the 1930s. Jerre Mangione, a young Sicilian-American who worked with the Federal Writers' Project, found himself dining at the White House and around the table were Jewish and Chinese individuals—all listening to the First Lady discuss race relations. Mangione, the son of a Rochester paperhanger, would return to the White House for a weekend with the Roosevelts, and Joseph Lash, son of a Jewish storekeeper, became a frequent guest.

Visits from average Americans increased while Pat Nixon was First Lady. She wanted as many people as possible to have the special thrill of receiving a personal invitation to the White House. During the first year of the Nixon presidency, a record-breaking 60,000 people got their names on guest lists at 1600 Pennsylvania Avenue. A dinner party on the South Lawn honoring returning prisoners of war drew thirteen hundred people, making it the largest such event ever held there. On Thanksgiving day, 225 elderly Washingtonians were bused in from all around the city to eat at the White House.

Pat Nixon also reached out to people in other ways. She refused to use a facsimile of her signature and paid the price for that decision by signing autographs for several hours each day. Tourists found her a warm hostess who sometimes hugged those who seemed a little frightened by the place. When one little boy objected that it could not be the President's House because there was no washing machine, the First Lady led him by the hand upstairs to see one.

No matter how determined the President and his family are to open the White House to everyone, the size of the nation dictates that only a tiny fraction can ever set foot inside. Television brings the mansion into the homes of most of the others. Harry Truman introduced the idea of a televised White House tour after gutting and rebuilding of the interior was completed in 1952, and Jacqueline Kennedy led television cameras through the public rooms a decade later. Tricia Nixon, the President's daughter, also consented to act as hostess for a televised tour of the mansion, and in 1990 George and Barbara Bush issued a public invitation to "the first live tour of the White House in over twenty-five years" on the television show *Prime Time Live*.

President Jimmy Carter helped stir a barbecue on the South Lawn.

★ ★ ★

Americans' vicarious "invasion" of the President's House began on the printed page over a century ago. As national magazines increased their circulation in the late nineteenth century and tried to appeal to more women readers, they hired women reporters. The subject of politicians' family life became a popular one. Emily Briggs, writing as "Olivia" for the *Philadelphia Press*, got her scoops from a White House steward, and other reporters relied on guests and employees to tell how things were done inside.

In 1873 a fictional "Aunt Mehitable" (pseudonym for Harriet Hazelton) began contributing a monthly column to *Godey's Lady's Book,* one of the biggest women's magazines. Taking the part of an uneducated country woman, "Aunt Mehitable" described in detail a visit to the Grant White House with its gold wallpaper and fancy

Harry Atwood landed an airplane on the White House lawn in 1911 after President Taft declined his invitation to go for a ride.

chandeliers. When she wrote how the First Lady was so "ugly" that she resorted to shuttered windows and gas lights in the middle of the afternoon to avoid scrutiny, readers could participate vicariously in both the glamour and the glee.

That same curiosity about White House families continued, even accelerated, in the twentieth century when electronic and print media competed among themselves to furnish the most information. Newspapers published details about every state dinner— the guest list, the menu, and what the President, First Lady, and honored guests wore. Even recipes for main dishes were sometimes included, along with a mention of the hour that the President went to bed.

Demands to share in the White House often appear boundless, extending even to using it for personal celebrations. A White House wedding might be considered the exclusive domain of those who reside or work there, but as late as 1944 one Navy Department stenographer with no particular connection to the presidential family wrote to Eleanor Roosevelt requesting to be married in the White House "on the 11th or 12th of this month." The First Lady's secretary was left the duty of declining. Refusals must be carefully phrased, like those of a renter objecting to a landlord's request, and Presidents make a point of acknowledging frequently their debt to the American people.

★★★

A loyal staff reinforces the White House's role as the People's House. Employees tend to think of themselves as servants of the nation, much as they would if they worked at any other public monument or government office. They often remain for decades, regardless of the turnover in Chief Executives and political parties, and in so doing they develop considerable expertise in how to run the White House.

In the 1960s when Lady Bird Johnson noted that the staff went on with its work no matter who the occupants were, she reiterated a point made by a reporter who wrote in 1909 that the President's House, with its thirty employees, "pretty much ran itself." In the 1920s, strong-willed Florence Harding, acknowledging that she felt somewhat superfluous, explained in a letter: "In this big house I do not have quite the same feeling of running the wheels myself as I

Barbara Bush conducts invited visitors through the Lincoln Bedroom.

President and Mrs. Kennedy talk with Pearl Buck and Robert Frost in the East Room after a dinner in honor of Nobel Prize winners.

did in a smaller establishment but I do keep my hand on the helm and give it a turn now and then."

Betty Ford, who assumed First Lady duties after the Nixon resignation in August 1974, learned that a state dinner had been planned for the next week. The Fords had not yet moved into the White House and had known nothing of the dinner plans. At first Mrs. Ford felt overwhelmed but then realized that "the White House is filled with people who can do anything—cook, bake, serve, design and hand-letter place cards, arrange flowers and choose music. All you have to do is know what you want and ask for it."

Presidential families seeking to impose their own tastes on White House management find that the establishment runs largely on rules of its own under the direction of a Chief Usher. That job gained in power because it has typically been held for many years by the same man. Irwin ("Ike") Hoover first came to the White House as an electrician in the spring of 1891 and he remained employed there a total of forty-two years, twenty of them as Chief Usher. Coincidentally, one President he served had the same family name (although the men were not relatives) and Lou Hoover insisted that he be addressed as "Mr. Usher" in order to avoid any confusion that might result from having two Mr. Hoovers in the same household. "Mr. Usher" Hoover was succeeded in 1933 by Howell G. Crimm, who served a remarkable twenty-four years.

The usher position started out as a kind of steward—someone who intercepted visitors and relayed their calling cards to the President's secretary. As early as the 1840s, the British term "usher" sometimes attached itself to this intermediary, who also took on the responsibility of approving food orders, accepting deliveries, and performing other household management tasks.

Lady Bird Johnson chose the Lincoln Bedroom for her meeting in April 1964 with poet Carl Sandburg (center) and photographer Edward Steichen (left).

203

President and Mrs. Reagan invite guests to join them in dancing at the White House.

By 1897 when the title "Chief Usher" became official, the job, as well as that of his assistants, was highly coveted. Ushers stood well above domestic servants—they dressed in frock coats during the day, worked closely with the First Lady, played with the President's children, and enjoyed the perquisites that naturally come to anyone with frequent access to a powerful person. From an office just inside the north entrance, they monitored all entrances and exits.

Ushers became enormously valuable to Presidents and their families, and when J. B. West published his account of his years as Chief Usher, he subtitled it *Upstairs at the White House: My Life with the First Ladies*. Presidents' wives repaid him with many compliments, and when he died, Jacqueline Kennedy Onassis made one of her rare intercessions with the Reagans to get special permission so that West could be buried in Arlington National Cemetery.

By the end of the White House's second century, the job of Chief Usher had become a demanding management position. The incumbent, Gary Walters, heads a staff of more than one hundred, and additional employees come in for special occasions such as state dinners or whenever unusual skills are required. The office of the Chief Usher, still situated inside the north entrance as it has been since the 1840s, boasts state-of-the-art technology; a computer screen flashes the location of any member of the President's family who is on White House grounds as well as the whereabouts of the President, in order to help coordinate activities occurring simultaneously in the mansion. All workers and visitors to the residence are cleared through the Chief Usher. If the White House were a city, he would be town manager.

Even lesser staff jobs have shown remarkable longevity, thus underlining the fact that the staff serves a nation rather than a particular President. Elizabeth Jaffray, hired as head housekeeper by Helen Taft in 1909, remained seventeen years and worked for four different families before leaving to write her book, *Secrets of the White House*. Isabella Hagner, the young War Department clerk employed at the White House in 1901 to help with the First Lady's correspondence, remained there eight years, resumed her job at the War Department during the Taft administration, and was re-

Dinner in the State Dining Room with President
Lincoln's portrait over the fireplace.

Chief Usher Gary Walters oversees the mansion's operation from an office inside the north entrance. Here he is shown in the ground-floor library.

called to the White House by Woodrow Wilson's wife in 1913. Her return was remarkable—the 1912 election had been a bitter three-way contest in which Wilson had defeated both the Republican nominee William Howard Taft and the insurgent Bull Moose candidate Theodore Roosevelt, but even the acrimony of that contest did not negate Hagner's value as secretary to the new First Lady.

The expertise of social secretaries and Chief Ushers might be offered as reason for keeping them on after their original employers have left, but strictly domestic workers have also remained through changes in administrations. One of Helen Taft's hirees, Maggie Rogers, came to work as a maid in 1909 and was still there when her daughter took a similar position twenty years later. Robert Taylor Smith from Wooster, Ohio, took a job as White House messenger in 1897 when he was a young man of twenty-two and stayed for fifty-two years; and Edmund Starling, who began working at the White House in 1914, boasted that he had known every President from Woodrow Wilson to Franklin Roosevelt.

Staff members learn to keep a low profile and respect privacy. Distinguished visitors, elaborate security arrangements, complex scheduling, and high pressure are all part of every day's work. On hand for the funeral of one President, they can assist more usefully at the next; present for one war, they can help to prepare the house for the next one.

After Pearl Harbor, those who had worked in the White House during the World War I years would recall how the American people looked to the presidential residence and its First Family as models of how to keep up morale. In 1917 Edith Wilson served "meatless" and "wheatless" meals and arranged for twenty Shropshire black-faced sheep to graze on the White House lawn. Then when the time came to shear them, she contributed to the war effort the $52,828 from the wool, which states competed among themselves to auction at the highest price. Rolling bandages for the Red Cross and chauffeuring soldiers around the capital, the First Lady might have been the wife of any CEO intent on helping her country. President Wilson's three daughters all joined in the effort. Margaret, the eldest, who was just starting a singing career, donated all her earnings to the war, and Jessie and Nellie rolled bandages and helped at servicemen's canteens.

White House Social Secretary Linda Faulkner briefs social aides, officers of the Armed Forces, on how to greet guests at the East Entrance and escort them to the state floor for lunch in the Family Dining Room.

Twenty-five years later, during World War II, First Lady Eleanor Roosevelt also spent a great deal of time and attention on the war effort and took much of her work on the road. Canceling the White House social season, she went off to inspect troops in England and the Pacific. Americans who looked to the White House for leadership during those years knew that the Roosevelt sons were all in uniform, and saw the President's house as just one more American residence that had sent its sons to fight.

★ ★ ★

In wartime or peace, the shrewdest Presidents remember that they occupy public property and hold a limited "lease" at 1600 Pennsylvania Avenue. Ever since the White House was built, Americans have demanded that it reflect their tastes, answer to their criticism, and serve as a model for the best that they themselves could become. A loyal staff maintains the mansion in the best possible condition—for the President and his family; for the national and world leaders who arrive to meet with the President; for the millions of average people who tour the public rooms or are invited as special guests; and, as a legacy, for the many generations still to come.

During its first two hundred years the stone walls of the White House have grown remarkably elastic, expanding to accommodate ever larger numbers of visitors, staff, and offices, as well as multiple roles and functions. Individual Presidents may call it home, but through two centuries it has remained the People's House—and its importance as a symbol of the American people has never diminished.

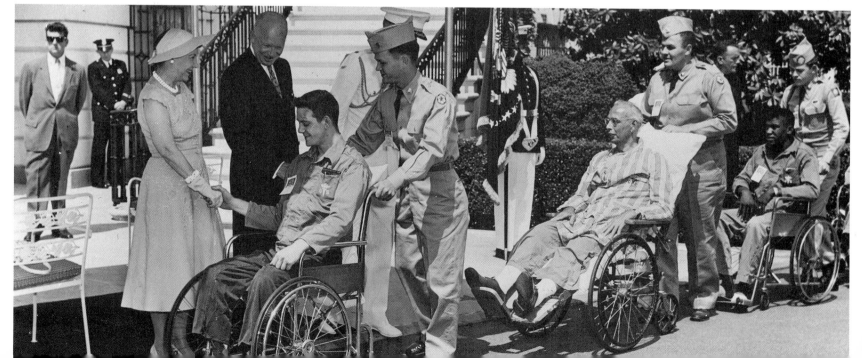

In May 1956, President Eisenhower and First Lady Mamie Eisenhower greeted veterans at a garden party on the South Lawn.

On his first full day in office,
President Bill Clinton welcomed
visitors to the Diplomatic Reception Room.
Vice President Al Gore is at the left.

While Americans seek a closer look inside,
Presidents and their families use the White House
as a special vantage point from which to view others.
Above: The Kennedy family is shown on
the South Balcony, November 13, 1963.
Below: Nearly three decades later, First Lady
Hillary Rodham Clinton stood on the same balcony,
eager to participate in a third century
of White House history.

PRESIDENTS OF THE UNITED STATES AND THEIR WIVES

	Years in Office		Years in Office
WASHINGTON, George (1732–1799) Martha Dandridge Custis Washington (1731–1802)	**1789–1797**	**MONROE,** James (1758–1831) Elizabeth Kortright Monroe (ca. 1763–1830)	**1817–1825**
ADAMS, John (1735–1826) Abigail Smith Adams (1744–1818)	**1797–1801**	**ADAMS,** John Quincy (1767–1848) Louisa Johnson Adams (1775–1852)	**1825–1829**
JEFFERSON, Thomas (1743–1826) Martha Wayles Skelton Jefferson (1748–1782)	**1801–1809**	**JACKSON,** Andrew (1767–1845) Rachel Donelson Robards Jackson (1767–1828)	**1829–1837**
MADISON, James (1751–1836) Dolley Payne Todd Madison (1768–1849)	**1809–1817**	**VAN BUREN,** Martin (1782–1862) Hannah Hoes Van Buren (1783–1819)	**1837–1841**

	Years in Office		Years in Office
HARRISON, William Henry (1773–1841) Anna Symmes Harrison (1775–1864)	**1841**	**HAYES,** Rutherford (1822–1893) Lucy Webb Hayes (1831–1889)	**1877–1881**
TYLER, John (1790–1862) Letitia Christian Tyler (1790–1842) Julia Gardiner Tyler (1820–1889)	**1841–1845**	**GARFIELD,** James (1831–1881) Lucretia Rudolph Garfield (1832–1918)	**1881**
POLK, James (1795–1849) Sarah Childress Polk (1803–1891)	**1845–1849**	**ARTHUR,** Chester (1829–1886) Ellen Herndon Arthur (1837–1880)	**1881–1885**
TAYLOR, Zachary (1784–1850) Margaret Smith Taylor (1788–1852)	**1849–1850**	**CLEVELAND,** Grover (1837–1908) Frances Folsom Cleveland (1864–1947)	**1885–1889** **1893–1897**
FILLMORE, Millard (1800–1874) Abigail Powers Fillmore (1798–1853)	**1850–1853**	**HARRISON,** Benjamin (1833–1901) Caroline Scott Harrison (1832–1892) Mary Lord Dimmick Harrison (1858–1948)	**1889–1893**
PIERCE, Franklin (1804–1869) Jane Appleton Pierce (1806–1863)	**1853–1857**	**McKINLEY,** William (1843–1901) Ida Saxton McKinley (1847–1907)	**1897–1901**
BUCHANAN, James (1791–1868) [never married]	**1857–1861**	**ROOSEVELT,** Theodore (1858–1919) Alice Lee Roosevelt (1861–1884) Edith Carow Roosevelt (1861–1948)	**1901–1909**
LINCOLN, Abraham (1809–1865) Mary Todd Lincoln (1818–1882)	**1861–1865**	**TAFT,** William Howard (1857–1930) Helen Herron Taft (1861–1943)	**1909–1913**
JOHNSON, Andrew (1808–1875) Eliza McCardle Johnson (1810–1876)	**1865–1869**	**WILSON, Woodrow (1856–1924)** Ellen Axson Wilson (1860–1914) Edith Bolling Galt Wilson (1872–1961)	**1913–1921**
GRANT, Ulysses (1822–1885) Julia Dent Grant (1826–1902)	**1869–1877**	**HARDING,** Warren (1865–1923) Florence Kling De Wolfe Harding (1860–1924)	**1921–1923**

	Years in Office
COOLIDGE, Calvin (1872–1933) Grace Goodhue Coolidge (1879–1957)	**1923–1929**
HOOVER, Herbert (1874–1964) Lou Henry Hoover (1874–1944)	**1929–1933**
ROOSEVELT, Franklin (1882–1945) Eleanor Roosevelt Roosevelt (1884–1962)	**1933–1945**
TRUMAN, Harry (1884–1972) Bess Wallace Truman (1885–1982)	**1945–1953**
EISENHOWER, Dwight (1890–1969) Mamie Doud Eisenhower (1896–1979)	**1953–1961**
KENNEDY, John (1917–1963) Jacqueline Bouvier Kennedy (1929–)	**1961–1963**
JOHNSON, Lyndon (1908–1973) Claudia (Lady Bird) Taylor Johnson (1912–)	**1963–1969**

	Years in Office
NIXON, Richard (1913–) Patricia Ryan Nixon (1912–1993)	**1969–1974**
FORD, Gerald (1913–) Elizabeth (Betty) Bloomer Warren Ford (1918–)	**1974–1977**
CARTER, Jimmy (1924–) Rosalynn Smith Carter (1927–)	**1977–1981**
REAGAN, Ronald (1911–) Jane Wyman Reagan (1914–) Nancy Davis Reagan (1921–)	**1981–1989**
BUSH, George (1924–) Barbara Pierce Bush (1925–)	**1989–1993**
CLINTON, Bill (1946–) Hillary Rodham Clinton (1947–)	**1993–**

President and Mrs. Hoover, accompanied by two of their grandchildren, greet a crowd gathered outside the South Portico.

FLOOR PLAN OF THE WHITE HOUSE

Ground Floor

G1   Library
*G2   Ground Floor Corridor
G3   Vermeil Room
G4   China Room
G5   Diplomatic Reception Room
G6   Map Room

First Floor

*F1   East Room
*F2   Green Room
*F3   Blue Room
F4   South Portico
*F5   Red Room
*F6   State Dining Room
F7   Family Dining Room
*F8   Cross Hall
*F9   Entrance Hall

*An asterisk marks rooms open to the public

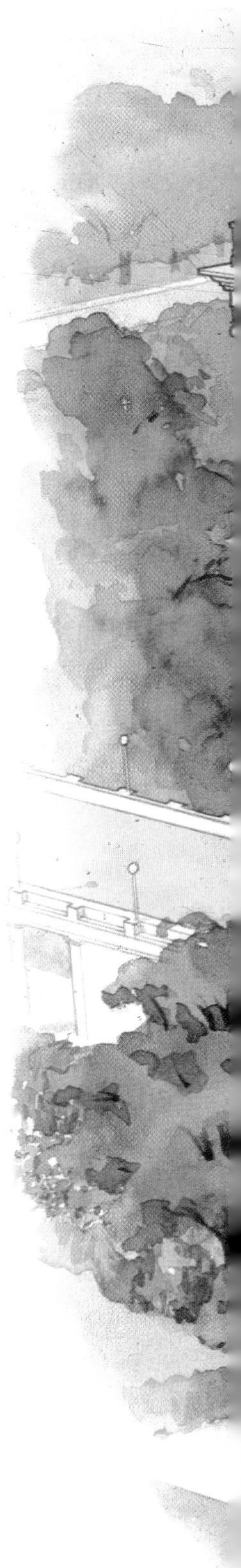

*F6 F7

*F9

*F8

*F5

*F3

*F2

F4

*F1

G6

G1

*G2

G4

G5

G3

Robert W. Nicholson

PHOTO CREDITS

Grateful acknowledgment is made to the sources whose photographs and illustrations appear on the following pages:

AP/Wide World Photos: 17, 30, 35, 49, 128, 209, 224
Harry Benson. Copyright © 1993 by Harry Benson: 210
Susan Biddle, The White House: 19, 25 (bottom), 74
Jimmy Carter Library: 44, 48 (top), 52 (top), 79, 86, 109, 120, 167, 170, 199
Corning Museum of Glass: 123, 150, 152, 155
Culver Pictures, Inc.: 38, 39, 62, 63
Dwight D. Eisenhower Library: 50, 77, 127, 208. Also courtesy of National Park Service: 77, 127, 208.
Gerald R. Ford Library: 22, 41, 45 (top), 52 (bottom), 54 (top), 76, 90, 112
Rutherford B. Hayes Presidential Center: 78, 158, 191, 196
Herbert Hoover Presidential Library-Museum: 53 (top), 92, 213
Houghton Library, Harvard University: 32, 84, 177
Lyndon B. Johnson Library: 4, 23 (top), 24, 37, 56, 65, 71, 102, 107, 125, 183, 203
John F. Kennedy Library: 20, 25 (top), 73, 91, 94, 95, 96, 101, 104, 119, 169, 202, 210
John Kordel, Metropolitan Singers/Greek Choral Society: 182
Library of Congress: 9, 11, 12, 13, 14, 15, 27, 29, 31, 33, 36, 46 (top), 47, 48 (bottom), 53 (bottom), 57, 58, 59, 60, 61, 67, 80, 81, 82, 83, 85, 116, 143, 144, 172, 173, 174, 175, 176, 179, 181, 188, 190, 192, 193, 200, 218, 220
National Archives: 34, 69, 186, 187
National Park Service: 16
The New York Times. Copyright © 1985 by The New York Times. Reprinted by permission: 98
Richard Nixon Library, National Archives: 115, 133, 198
Y.R. Okamoto, Lyndon B. Johnson Library: 66, 217
Carol T. Powers, The White House: 21, 184 (top), 201, 223
Ronald Reagan Library, National Archives: 97, 111, 204, back endsheet
Franklin D. Roosevelt Library: 45 (bottom), 46 (bottom), 55, 93, 118, 165, 194. Also courtesy of UPI/Bettmann: 45 (bottom), 165.
David Valdez, The White House: 51, 54 (bottom), 70, 184 (bottom), 185
White House Historical Association: front endsheet, 2, 7, 23 (bottom), 40, 42, 43, 89, 100, 110, 122, 131, 134, 137, 138, 139, 141, 145, 146, 147, 148, 149, 151, 156, 157, 159, 161, 162, 164, 195, 205, 206, 207, 214–15. Also courtesy of National Geographic: front endsheet, 7, 43, 89, 164, 207. Also courtesy of Leet-Melbrook, Inc.: 42.

FURTHER READINGS

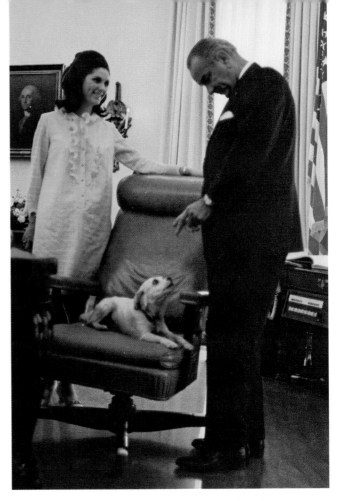

President Lyndon Johnson let one of his dogs try out his desk chair in July 1968, after he had announced that he would not run for another term.

Kirk, Elise K. *Music at the White House*. Chicago: University of Illinois Press, 1986.

Klapthor, Margaret. *Official White House China: 1789 to the Present*. Washington, D.C.: Smithsonian Institution Press, 1975.

Ryan, William, and Desmond Guinness. *The White House: An Architectural History*. New York: McGraw-Hill Book Company, 1980.

Seale, William. *The President's House*. 2 vols., Washington D.C.: White House Historical Association, 1986.

Spillman, Jane Shadel. *White House Glassware*. Washington, D.C.: White House Historical Association, 1989.

White House Historical Association. *The White House: An Historic Guide*. 17th ed. Washington, D.C.: White House Historical Association, 1991.

White House Historical Association. *The Living White House*. 8th ed. Washington, D.C.: White House Historical Association, 1987.

First Lady Grace Coolidge, famous for her fondness for animals, is shown with her dog Rob Roy.

INDEX

(page numbers in **boldface** refer to illustrations)

President Harding's dog inside the White House shortly after his owner died in August 1923.

President George Bush and new grandchild, Charles Walker Bush.

223

President Harry Truman tried out the new White House bowling alley— but did not change his shoes.